FISHER IN THE HILLS

FISHER IN THE HILLS

A Season in Galloway

written and illustrated by

Robin Ade

ANDRE DEUTSCH

First published in 1985 by
André Deutsch Limited
105 Great Russell Street London WC1

The drawings on pages 33 (lower) and
119 are by Kevin Ade.

ISBN 0 233 97570 5

Phototypeset by Falcon Graphic Art Limited
Wallington, Surrey
Printed in Great Britain by
St Edmundsbury Press
Bury St. Edmunds, Suffolk

Contents

For my parents

Introduction

It happend that on my first visit to south-west Scotland I was looking for a place to settle. I liked the atmosphere of Galloway, a little publicized area which, in spite of its proximity to the Borders and the main routes north, appeared to be a relatively unspoilt part of the country. I was fortunate in that I had friends there willing to accept a new neighbour on their smallholding and it was not long before I returned to base myself in a caravan in the high hills beyond the village of Carsphairn.

My first summer passed in a succession of idyllic ramblings along the unfrequented waters which lay all round me. For me the hills were filled with magic, and in the years which followed I became familiar with the sights and sounds of nature in a way which recalled childhood. For a trout fisher the Galloway hills left little to be desired; I fished when and where I fancied, and the problems of finding enough work in a remote area to sustain my activities were compensated for by the satisfactions of spending most of my time in the Scottish countryside. When odd jobs or seasonal work failed to materialize I revived my interest in drawing and painting.

The isolation of our valley is one of its charms, yet, with the passage of time, a sad story of depopulation has come to light. Old people who were born and raised here sometimes come to visit and we live among the ghosts of a traditional community which died out less than twenty years ago. The final blow to this, as to many another rural community throughout Scotland, came with the so-called 'second clearances', an ongoing process by which shepherds and other residents of the hills make way for blocks of sitka spruce. Efforts to integrate farming with forestry have yet to begin and, since today's population of the upland half of Great Britain would hardly fill a small town, there are too few people left in these areas now to influence public policy on such developments.

While depopulation continues the environment itself has come under new threats. In the case of acid rain threat has become reality, and a serious toll has been taken of Galloway's rivers and lochs. Those I visit have not as yet been adversely affected, and it has therefore been possible to write this book, an account of one fishing season, with the trout still in a

healthy state. To the angler I apologize that the story is not, as it could easily have been, concerned only with fishing. I hope that he enjoys it nevertheless, and that others too will find it readable. Of the many people who have contributed to this book I would like to acknowledge the special assistance given by my neighbours at Carsphairn, Stephen Drummond Sedgewick, William Bulloch, S. Khan and particularly my wife Aletta.

Carsphairn
Easter, 1985

Then come, bonnie lassie, and climb the hill heartie,
The pleasures at hand let us share and enjoy;
Belyve something new might arrive to divert ye,
In shade o' great Cairnsmore that towers to the sky.

From 'Frae the Heather' by Thomas Murray

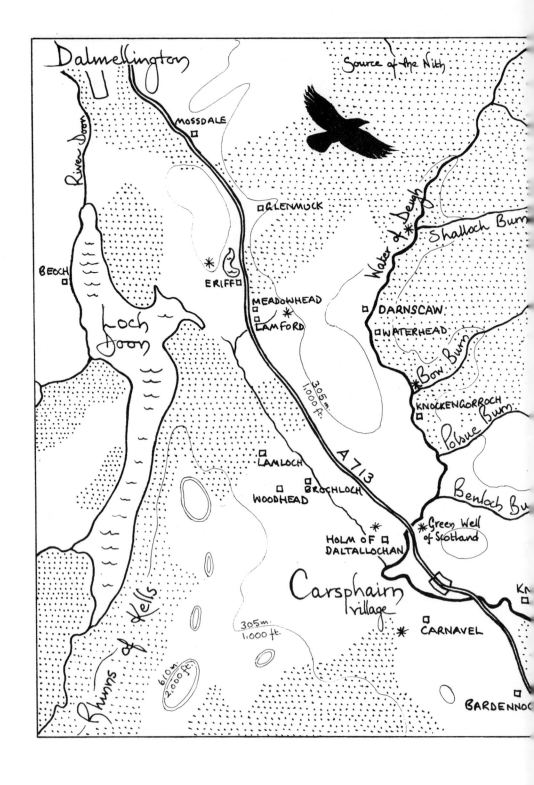

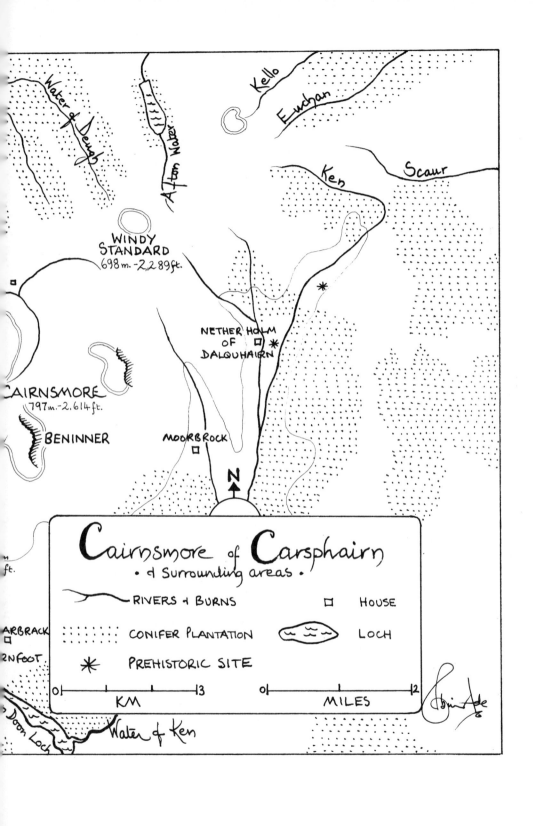

Water of Deugh

Kello

Euchan

Afton Water

Ken

Scaur

WINDY
STANDARD
698m. - 2,289ft.

NETHER HOLM
OF
DALQUHAIRN

CAIRNSMORE
797m. - 2,614ft.

BENINNER

MOORBROCK

N

ARBRACK

2NFOOT

Doon Loch

Water of Ken

Cairnsmore of Carsphairn
• & Surrounding areas •

RIVERS & BURNS   ☐   HOUSE

CONIFER PLANTATION   LOCH

✳   PREHISTORIC SITE

0   3   0   2

KM   MILES

CHAPTER ONE

Winter's End

On the first of March there was a thaw in the snow which had built up during ten days of south-easterly winds. The ice rings on the boulders of the river by our door began to melt and there was a touch of warmth in the air. Within days new sounds could be heard in the valley, the ringing calls of curlew and oystercatcher returning from the coast, and on the eleventh the frogs came out of their winter sleep. Their soft croakings, as they gathered in company, rose from the snow-edged margins of ditches and pools around the farm.

Towards the end of the month a day dawned on which it was no longer possible to ignore the signs. It came in softly from the south, bringing with it enough warmth to hint at activity among the wild trout of the little burn which joins the river not far upstream. These fish feed more freely in early spring than those of the river, and most years the first of the season come from its stony little pools.

From its source several miles above on Cairnsmore, the Bow Burn is shaped by the granite boulders which line its course. The last two miles wind back and forth between steep heather-topped banks, beyond which a forest of young coni-fers spreads over the lower hills. On this early spring day the more distant, higher hills, their smooth surfaces still shining with the sandy yellow of winter, contrasted sharply with the dark mass of spruce and fir below.

The sensation of walking the banks again was a strange one, for the long-remembered features of the landscape had a newness about them. There was an air of rebirth in the familiar scene viewed with new eyes, and a simple curiosity towards nature as a whole vied with the serious business of catching the first trout. I walked up past the little rowan-studded ravine which marks the entrance of the burn into the main valley. The high banks open out above here and, passing the old nesting site of the raven, I came to the first little pool. The rod handled stiffly on the first cast and the small worm rolled back down the stream-bed towards me without in-

terception. A few casts into this pool and the run above
limbered my rod arm and also let me know that the trout were
not active enough to go for fast-moving bait.

I approached the next pool, marked by its small stand of
native trees, with care. It looked at first sight too small to hold
much, but my neighbour Bill and I had long ago discovered
that this, the Hazel Pool, has unusual properties. For some
reason not apparent from the topography of the stream-bed it
holds several fair fish, including one or two over the eight-
inch average size. Sometimes it offers a feeding fish when the
rest of the water is dead and more than once it has given up
the first trout of the season.

I moved carefully around and above it, cut down to the burn
and crept among the stream-side boulders to a point above the
pool. I dropped the worm straight into the white water at the
neck and stripped out line as it raced downstream. When it
reached the tail I took the rod over to the left, pulling the bait
out of the current and letting it settle gently into the shallow
eddy under the near bank. There was no response, and after
allowing it to lie a few seconds I twitched the bait gently
towards me. I repeated the cast and began to wonder if the
effect of the sun on the icy waters of the burn had failed to
warm it enough for the trout to feed. Last year, the only fish of
my first visit had come from here when the water was rising
rapidly with cold snowmelt from the slopes of the Cairnsmore,
nearly a thousand feet above. Today, there was little snow on
the hills and the water was not particularly cold. My delibera-
tions were interrupted by a sudden tightening of the line
across the surface of the water. The rod-arm reflex returned in
a flash and I dropped the tip, letting the fish move off. This
pause, the bait-fisher's special moment, has an added sus-
pense when the bite is the first of the season. I tightened
gently, then pulled hard. The line went taut and the rod
jumped with the electric thrill of a hooked fish – a golden flash
as it twisted and ran, a hard haul on the rod, and nine inches
of bejewelled burn trout lay shimmering on the bank. I
dispatched it, with my best wishes for the hereafter, by
clasping it above the tail and bringing its head down sharply
on the nearest rock. I then laid it down to admire its colours for
the few short moments before they began to fade. It was a nice
fish for this small water and, though still showing slim winter
flanks, it was in fit shape. Green-backed, a row of light orange
spots running down its lateral line, its brightness was en-

hanced by the soft blue parr-marks which the burn trout retain throughout life.

Having found one fish feeding, I continued upstream in the hope of taking another two or three to make up a family meal. The next spot, the Ash Pool, is another good one, twice the size of the Hazel Pool. I often expect it to yield a half-pounder, but apart from a couple of possibles hooked and lost, it has not given up a big one. The best spot is behind a large rock at the near side of the pool, and today I moved in cautiously and cast a worm a foot or so beyond it. The slack line, lying across the top of the rock, immediately gave a sharp jerk and I hooked and landed an eight-incher. The evening meal was now half in the bag.

Above the Ash Pool the burn runs down wide, broken and shallow. There are lots of trout here, for the stones provide lairs aplenty, but they are mostly small, and only the few deeper pockets are likely to be worth fishing. I worked through this section rapidly without touching a fish and moved round the next bend towards the Fly Pool. This is one of the few pools large enough to cast a fly over comfortably, its ten-yard run being almost free of projecting stones except towards the tail. It is also one of the few to produce an occasional half-pounder. Today, however, its trout were dour and I made several casts without a sign of one.

Sooner or later during the course of this first spring walk I expect to meet one of the larger wild animals which live in this little valley almost undisturbed. Though anticipated, the meeting always comes as a surprise. Even if the animal is standing openly in the middle distance, looking like its field-guide image, in the first moments of encounter the personality of the creature asserts itself before the mind moves to label it with some familiar name.

This year my first encounter came just after I left the Fly Pool. The narrow deer-path which follows the stream climbs a small bank and opens onto a wide bend. At the top I paused suddenly as two big, reddish animals came twisting and turning along the bank towards me. Long, slim and very low to the ground, they were engaged in a running battle. Two or three times they rolled over, locked together in silent combat, moving up fast without seeing me, and at a distance of a few yards I recognized them as two big foxes: a lanky one with a patchy grey coat pursued by a sleek red animal with a white-tipped tail. They scrambled off the bank into the stream and continued the struggle, spray flying as they turned and twisted across the shallow water. Reaching the far side they raced up the high bank into the conifers, appeared again further along, and ran back down to the stream in front of me, where they slowed down and loped off up the other bank, still oblivious to my presence.

I followed the course of the burn up towards another ravine which marks the boundary of the lower valley. Familiarity with a water often leads to fishing only the known and trusted spots, a habit I try to avoid by watching for places as yet untried. Today this paid off when I caught an eight-incher by letting the worm run down with the current across a seemingly barren shallow. I walked across the stream afterwards and discovered a small, deep run alongside a boulder, invisible from the bank I usually walked up but large enough to give cover to this fish.

Around the next bend the high banks of the little valley close in until they reach the dark rock walls of the upper ravine. The air between them was still, and in the sunrays filtering down I saw some early mayflies, tiny creatures dancing like slow sparks over the water.

The waterfall at the head of the gorge is a familiar place and an excellent fishing spot. I rested a minute on the smooth ledge beside its lip, then threaded a small worm onto my hook and lowered it gently into the wall of water. The fall took it with a snatch and several yards of line whipped through my hands into the turbulence below. I guided the bait to the edge of the heavy current and immediately came a fast tug: a pause, a strike and a small trout flew out of the water and over the fall. Two further casts followed the same pattern, and I had three fish before the bait was left alone.

The meal being secured, I left the rod on the ledge and leapt across the fall. There is a rowan tree on the other side notable for its silver stem and, in the autumn, red berries of a striking brilliance. To the right is a small patch of almost even ground, a good camping area sheltered by high banks with the stream only feet away. There is also fuel, a sparse commodity in these hills, in the form of the dead lower branches of the rowans clinging to the sides of the ravine below.

Above the waterfall there is a dramatic change of scenery. The banks drop away and the wide vista of a remote upland valley opens up ahead. On either side the hills rise steeply; to the left, a last ragged patch of young conifers straggles out across a large smooth slope, and on the right there is the dark, rounded mass of the Cairnsmore, its deceptive heights concealing more than they reveal.

The upper valley holds memories, not only of fishing trips, but of walks in the solitude of the hills. There is a special character in the shapes of the Galloway hills, a subtle mould of power and tranquillity. Their smooth curves look water-worn, as if they once belonged to an undersea world, and they were in fact ground down from previously immense heights by the great glaciers of successive ice ages. Here there are no sharp nunatak peaks, the rocky spikes which once rose above the ice sheets and which are a common feature in the Highlands to the north.

The smoothness of their slopes, however, is misleading, for a close approach reveals a multitude of worlds hidden in their gentle faces. The Cairnsmore, for instance, has great stretches of boulder fields, unexpected valleys, peat bogs, rocky outcrops and numerous hidden waterways tucked away in its ample mass. The Bow Burn rises amid a tangle of granite blocks on one of its remoter slopes.

Solitude in this sort of wilderness has a profound effect on the mind. The first day of a hill walk brings that initial exhilaration of being out in the wilds, a fresh feeling which offsets the mental preoccupations which tend, even here, to crowd the mind. A strict survival sense must be maintained from the start, for a badly wrenched ankle on a wet and windswept hillside can lead to hypothermia and death within hours. A camping place which is sheltered from wind and rain should be found in good time, before darkness falls. Ideally there should be fuel nearby, for not only does a wood or peat fire create a centre of entertainment, but it gives far more light and warmth than a camping stove. In summer it can also be a necessary defence against the swarms of midges.

On the second day out the solitary traveller, having adapted to the open air, is able to accept his environment more freely. The body adjusts to changing temperatures faster and the systems of survival carried on the back become familiar with use. Physical conditions permitting, the next development is an inner one. The mental preoccupations of yesterday now assume an overwhelming presence: the people at home, instead of being left behind, will often become part of the baggage. Interminable mental conversations are carried on: as the sense of solitude deepens the more real the fantasies

become. However, the rituals of survival are so immediate in these surroundings that the activities required for a day's walk should give the mind a chance to clear itself of its overload.

If the traveller has been able to control his thoughts and his physical situation the third day should produce a new experience again: a clear-mindedness which makes for a heightened enjoyment of the environment. It is this clarity, however long it may take to arrive, which makes such journeys worthwhile.

It is an odd fact that there are now more remote areas in Scotland for wilderness walks than there have been for centuries. The hills are still being depopulated and the wild areas becoming wilder. New forestry replaces traditional farming communities with seasonal labour forces, and the trees create a wilderness of their own. The hard-working hill shepherds are disappearing, and their houses, if not near a road, are left to dereliction. There is a typical ruined cottage in the upper

'The Flower of Craig Tarsen and the Horror of Craig Horn' are the first lines of a shepherd's poem which refer respectively to the elegant, south-facing spur on Dugland Hill on the left, and the

valley beyond the waterfall, right under a distant shoulder of
the Cairnsmore. Its location is idyllic, surrounded on all sides
by awesome views, but it is miles from any road or other
habitation and it is over fifty years since Bert MacAdam, the
last shepherd, moved out.

The burn runs nearby, smaller now but with a few good
pools. People who remember it long ago say that these pools
once produced the Bow Burn's biggest trout, a pound and
more in weight. The burn was fished regularly in those days
and, as in many another small water, the size of trout declined
along with the dwindling interest of fishers. Today, occasional
heron and mink are the only predators of the large numbers of
tiny trout which fill these distant pools.

Back below the waterfall the numbers of trout are kept down
by a large population of mink. Although still numerous, the
fish are of a better average size than on unpredated streams of

*shadowy north-facing shoulder of the Cairnsmore on the right with
its tombstone-like rock formations. The Clennoch appears as a dot
between the two.*

the stony kind, where lairs and spawning beds are so abundant that the food supply is used to feed large populations of small fish rather than a smaller population of larger ones.

Today, after viewing the upper valley, I returned to collect my rod from the waterfall ledge. The afternoon sun, which had left the hills and their inhabitants in a strange sort of daze, was setting into a soft pink cloudbank. I returned rapidly downstream, stopping only when I reached the lower pools for a brief cast in each. Wild creatures, unaware of my presence, started their dusk routines. A kestrel flew within feet of me before alighting in his nightspot on the big ash. A deer barked from the steep bank behind and, turning, I saw a big roebuck silhouetted above it; for a long moment the beast remained poised against the sky, legs curled tightly in the climax of a great leap.

There is a big pool on the lower burn which I had ignored on the walk out since its placid length usually fishes as poorly as the larger river pools during daylight hours. Now, however, I saw rises breaking the reflection of the surface, and as I came in above it a good fish rose confidently beside a jutting ledge at the neck. This is the place where I had ended a memorable summer spate-catch, twenty-seven fish in under two hours, with a brace of half-pounders. Here, too, Bill once caught a three-quarter-pounder on a fly in a similar spate.

I cast a fat worm over the ledge and watched the bow of loose line curving up to the rod-tip. At the far end of the pool a pair of mallards came in with a whirr of wings and a long splash. I waved my arms to scare them off but they could not see me, and then the pale moth-like shape of an owl drifted over just above. I looked back to the water but my eye was caught instead by the dark shape of a roe deer, this time a doe, coming down the steep bank opposite. She approached within a few yards, leapt from a spur onto a mid-stream rock and again to my bank, where she started to graze. I finally turned my attention back to the line, but as I did it jumped and there was a splash beyond the ledge. I raised the rod and felt the resistance of a good fish, the seventh of the day and, at ten inches long, the largest.

'Over the hills and a long way off
The wind will blow my top-knot off'

<small>CHILDREN'S RHYME</small>

CHAPTER TWO

Stillwater Spring

April brought with it a long spell of settled weather, cold at night but with fine, sunny days. Outdoor activities on the farm now started in earnest as final preparations were made in the gardens and early seeds sown. Our neighbour's first lambs arrived at Easter, and the lambing season brought the shepherd out daily to his flocks on the open hill across the river. Bill, whose work on the rebuilding of an old drystone dyke on the Cairnsmore had been interrupted all winter by hard weather, took advantage of the fine spell to complete a long stretch.

New birds continued to arrive. A pair of missel thrushes settled at the farm, wheatears appeared on the moor, and sandpipers came to nest on the shingle banks along the river. Green shoots appeared under bleached tussocks along the valley floor, and the new growth of grass on the farm felt the running feet of children playing freely outside after long winter months indoors.

April also saw the start of regular fishing trips. At this time the hill lochs are at their best, and the patchy early fishing on the river is often neglected in favour of a walk to some favourite stillwater. Around the farm itself the only stillwaters are the peat pools along our wee garden burn. They were constructed in the form of a miniature fish farm but have been taken over by the native flora and fauna including small trout, frogs, newts, a fine display of swamp and water plants, some exotic insects, and an occasional mallard or heron. From March to June these pools are dominated by the spawning activities of the frogs, their dark heads raised over masses of eggs, and a visit to the garden is often accompanied by their crooning background chorus. When approached they dive from sight and, like the trout, their sharp eyes pick out movement a long way off. But unlike brown trout, they soon grow accustomed to human presence. At the nearest pool, just above our waterhole, a new group of spawning frogs often allows one to approach within feet after two or three days. They will get

23

used to an immobile figure beside them almost immediately; this is the hunting tactic of the heron, the success of whose early morning visits is evident from the frog remains he leaves behind him on the banks.

Frogspawn laid in the pools in March usually sits for weeks before developing into tadpoles and after heavy frosts the clumps on the surface are marked with the white dots of dead eggs. In May and June, however, the eggs often develop immediately and the whole process from egg to tiny frog takes place in little more than a month. The wriggling masses of tadpoles which fill the pools are easy prey for the aquatic predators, including trout, big diving beetles and the monstrous larvae of both diving beetles and dragonflies, two of the new creatures which appeared in the pools soon after they were dug.

The nearest natural stillwater is nearly two miles away. It is a shallow, wind-blown lochan high on a Cairnsmore shoulder, not far from the top of Bill's mile-long stretch of wall. At eighteen hundred feet, its subarctic environment does not sustain the wealth of plant and insect life of the garden pools a thousand feet below, and its tiny outlet stream is too steep to allow trout up to it.

This lochan is the only permanent pool on the Cairnsmore, but the Rhinns of Kells to the west hold stillwaters in profusion. A fine view of these hills can be had from the lochan shoulder, their peaks fading away like wavecrests towards the distant ocean. Lochs, burns, cascades and waterfalls glitter among them, a sparkling pattern of jewels which shimmer and fade with the changing light. Most of them hold wild trout in large numbers and, although the average size is small, the larger waters or those with limited spawning burns often hold some bigger ones. A few of the smaller lochs may, like the Cairnsmore lochan, have outlet streams which are inaccessible to fish and some have never seen the rings of a rising trout. A few of these are stocked by hill shepherds or people from outlying villages and, although the old practice of stocking remote barren waters is now on the decline, stories are still told of these secret places and their sometimes legendary trout.

The rarest type of wild trout loch is, naturally, the one which meets the angler's ideal of large numbers of big trout. Unlikely though it may seem, such waters do exist. Occasionally nature produces, in some bleak hill loch, a trout fishery of such quality that all the resources of fisheries' science would find it hard to duplicate. The location of these places is known to few people and when Bill and I, through a curious chain of events, discovered one of them, it was through a man who had inherited from his father a lifelong relationship with it.

Alec, its protector, had taken me up to the loch on a bright April day several years ago and on that first trip he had told me about the fishing. Trout under a pound in weight were rare and he had, in company with his father, taken up to forty fish a day during years when the water was at its best. It was a difficult place to approach, being surrounded by a broad belt of rushes, lilies and quaking bog. The folding dinghy which Alec carried on his back was the only means of covering it effectively.

An hour's walk into the hills had brought us near to the edge of the plateau where the loch lay, and Alec stopped by an old wall, removed a stone, and took out a kettle. We continued on over the last saddle, and there below us was a small, windswept disc of water surrounded by bare hills. It hardly looked the kind of place to hold big trout. We walked down to the near side of it, where Alec produced from under the bank some small dried bricks of peat, lit a fire, filled his kettle from the loch, and, with an air of familiar ritual, settled it atop the slow-burning mound.

After tea he put up his rod, attached a cast of three big traditional flies to the line, prepared the dinghy, and put out onto the water. The trout were slow to co-operate and we both had a session without hooking one. After an hour or two Alec, fishing against the lilies on the far side, finally had an offer and I saw from the arc in his rod that he was into a good fish. He held it hard and it was not long before he netted it, dispatched it, and paddled back over. The fish was a finely proportioned male, over a pound in weight and with a distinctive set of markings. Its sides were thickly covered with large, clear spots, some a vivid red; behind each eye there was a great patch of emerald, and its broad back was coloured a strong olive green. That night I found that the eating quality of its bright orange flesh was, as Alec had predicted, of the best.

A fortnight after that first visit I went up to the loch again, this time with Bill. We arrived late, planning to stay the night at the lochside and to fish at dusk and dawn. We lacked a dinghy, however, and had to search the margins for a place from which we could cast a line. The new season's growth of rushes had barely started, but we found only one small area where they were sparse enough to fish across. We fished spinners into the twilight and within minutes a fish took Bill's little Devon minnow. It leapt hard just beyond the rushes but Bill held the rod high and after a few minutes he steered the fish through the rushes to where I was able to reach down, grab it behind the head, and flip it up onto the bank. It was another male, again in fine condition, but this one was nearer two pounds in weight.

My turn to hook a trout came the following morning. We rose early to find the loch glassy calm, but by the time we had brewed tea several heavy rises had broken its surface. One trout rose near our fishable spot, and after breakfast we walked over there. A half-hour's spinning brought no response, and the early morning rises petered out except for a single fish which periodically showed away to the left. I looked at the bank beyond it and wondered if it was possible to get within casting range. The fish was rising in a clear patch between lily beds quite close to the edge, but the bank itself, which looked innocent enough from a distance, I knew to consist of a forty-yard band of treacherous quaking bog.

Giving in to temptation, I set off round the shore and stepped carefully onto the grassy surface. The whole area trembled violently and my boots sank deep with every step, but the skin of interwoven vegetation held firm and I moved slowly across to within a rod-length of the open water. At this point the fish rose again, straight ahead and only a few yards out. I had mounted a large natural minnow on my rod and, stripping a few yards of line off the reel, I cast the unweighted bait gently out beyond the lilies and began to retrieve it in slow pulls just under the surface. Nothing happened, and after another couple of casts I called over to Bill that Devon minnows were obviously more appealing to these trout than the real thing. This, it seemed, was the signal for my fish; the line stopped suddenly halfway to the bank, I tightened, and the surface of the loch was shattered by the leap of another good trout. Absorbed in the fight, I hardly noticed that the bog had reached my knees, but the grassy skin held firm and so did the trout, a delicately proportioned female of a pound and a quarter, which I eventually landed by drawing it onto the flush edge of the bog.

In the years which followed we learned something of the qualities which make this loch so unusual. The most obvious of these is that the numbers of fish in it are low enough for all of them to grow large without unduly diminishing the food supply. The loch has no inlet streams and, since the only small fish to be taken from it are caught in September, it appears that its annual stock consists of the limited number of trout which find their way up the swampy outlet during the autumn. A restriction in numbers will result in big fish from almost any natural water but it would not explain the relative profusion of big fish which this loch produces. An unusually abundant food source is the only way a high hill loch can grow such numbers, and this happens only when the water is robbed of its normally high acidity. This particular loch lies in a small patch of limestone and, in addition to a broad range of aquatic insects, it contains pea mussels, rare creatures in acid waters. A further reason for fast trout growth in any water is year-round feeding, and judging by the excellent condition of its fish as early on as March, it could be that the springs which feed this loch keep the water temperature high enough for trout to remain actively feeding during at least part of the winter. These qualities may combine to create an exceptional fishing water in an unlikely place, but the ecological balance of any such water is likely to be delicate. Some small change in the outlet stream, for instance, may allow too many fish to enter, and the food animals, once depleted by an overpopulation of trout, may never be able to re-establish themselves in their former abundance.

Although this loch has not yet suffered such an overpopulation, Alec told me of two occurrences which caused a severe fall in numbers. The first was the 'discovery' of the loch by a group of anglers – in this situation usually called poachers – who proceeded to deplete the trout as fast as possible without regard for the future. They took some fine fish, including three- and four-pounders, but when most of the big fish had gone they left the loch to its former obscurity. The trout recovered their numbers but in recent years they have been affected again, this time by a lack of new autumn arrivals from the outlet stream.

Alec had spoken of two smaller waters on the same plateau which we visited on later trips. One is a mere boghole, so small that it can be easily covered from one fishing position. The second is a lochan about fifty yards wide with a small patch of goat willows at one end and a large population of small, free-biting trout.

This year I planned to meet Alec and his son for another April visit. The walk-up passed quickly as I was travelling light on a familiar route. The treeless hills were still pale with the bleached grass of last year, and a desert-like landscape reflected the steady glare of the sun. Blackface sheep started up at my approach, and two black-backed gulls appeared and followed with harsh calls until I was clear of their nesting

territory. After some time I reached a derelict shepherd's cottage and stopped briefly to collect firewood, dead boughs from the stand of large sycamores which still surrounds the ruin. Then, climbing down to the left, I walked along the edge of a swampy, sedge-filled hollow and joined the old stone wall which runs up over the last saddle.

The little loch shone blue under the sun and from above its calm water looked welcoming in spite of the bleakness of its surroundings. There was no sign of Alec, but down at the lochside I found the remains of a fire and knew he was probably not far away. The fishable place of past visits was again relatively free of marginal rushes, and as I set up the tackle I saw rises out on the loch. The trout were taking big brown mayflies drifting across the water on the light breeze, but the rises looked like those of small fish.

Presently Alec and his son appeared carrying rods and dinghy. I went over to meet them, and as we stood talking on the bank there was a whirr of wings and we were joined by a white pigeon. 'There'll be a falcon about,' said Alec, and we turned to see a large, grey bird with pointed wings and long tail disappear over the saddle: a peregrine. Above the loch there is a rocky bluff where these birds watch for prey: mountain hares, grouse, and the racing pigeons whose air

lanes take them through peregrine country. After the falcon had gone Alec told me of another incident here a few days before. He was fishing from the bank when there was a heavy thump in the air above and a pigeon dropped into the water in front of him. The bird had been struck by a peregrine but was not seriously injured; Alex scooped it up in his landing net, and it recovered enough to be released on his way home. He has a photograph recording another incident: it shows his father holding a day's catch from another hill loch, consisting not of trout, but of a peregrine-killed pigeon. The one which had just joined us was more fortunate. It had a few feathers knocked out, but within a couple of hours it recovered enough to leave of its own accord.

As Alec lit the fire I looked at his morning's catch: a dozen small fish taken on the wet fly, mostly from the lochan. And what of the trout from the main loch? 'This came from here early on,' he said, pointing to a beautifully marked fish, the largest of the catch but still under half a pound. 'What about the big ones?' I asked. 'There don't seem to be many new fish getting up to the loch now,' he answered, 'and last year I put in eighty-three wee ones from the boghole.' So this was the reason for the presence of the small fish. 'They seem to be growing well,' Alec said, pointing to the larger trout, which was remarkably plump for the time of year and already two or three times the weight of the fish from the boghole.

On the far side a couple of larger fish were rising. After tea Alec went across in the dinghy to try for them, and his son and I walked over to the point to fish our worms. The big mayfly hatch had slowed down, but one or two trout were still rising within casting range. We caught two in quick succession – fat, colourful fish, the larger one nearly half a pound, and both already possessing distinctive markings: large, clear spots and delicate green backs.

We fished for a while but caught no more trout. The rise petered out and a strengthening north-west wind started a heavy ripple across the loch. Alec returned for tea without a fish; he had missed three before making the common fly-fisher's discovery that the point of his hook was missing.

It was now mid-afternoon and after tea my companions set off home. The sun still glared down and the only sounds were the cries of curlews and the continuous song of skylarks. The loch had, temporarily at least, lost its appeal and I decided it was time to fish the lochan.

I skirted the left bank of the loch and continued up the low, tussocky rise at the far end. From here I could see the glittering blue disc of the lochan and the still bare branches of its little willows. Its green margins looked deceptively easy to approach but I knew that this water too was surrounded by quaking bog. I knew also of a small area at the far end where the surface skin was thick enough to stand on without sinking and from which I could cast over the marginal pondweed. I walked down the slope, across a splashy strip of bog, and down to the fishing spot. The wind, blowing from behind, enabled me to cover half of the surface from this one position. There was a good rise of trout along the margins and I was optimistic as I threaded a small worm on the hook. I cast my worm and cork-float out towards the left-side margin, letting the wind put a bow in the line before allowing it to drift across the surface.

Almost immediately the float vanished. I paused, struck and felt nothing. The worm appeared untouched, so I cast again, and this time the wave took the cork out in a long arc before it bobbed and went down. Again there was no resistance on the strike, and I now prepared to wait for my catch for I knew the problems of connecting with trout when they are in a nibbling mood. Clever adjustments of the worm and hook make no difference as the fish simply grab the bait lightly in their lips, without taking it further down, just as they do when coming short to the fly. I went through the ritual of bait adjustment anyhow, and missed several more fish at various points on the drift before finally hooking a wee one against the far margin.

At one point my fishing was disturbed by a splash from behind, and I turned to see an orange weasel swimming towards me across a shallow puddle. It came on across the moss with a fast, snake-like movement, straight to the tackle bag at my feet. It took a sniff at the bag, recoiled in surprise, looked up at me, and continued on its way to the water where , slipping smoothly in, it swam off along the margin like a mink.

The sun was now dropping low, the wind began to falter and slacken, and trout started to rise confidently all over the surface. Now at last I began to hook them, eight- and nine-inchers which put up a remarkable struggle for their size and needed a hard, fast haul to bring them up over the pondweed.

I fished on and, from the middle of the loch, caught a ten-inch trout, the largest I had seen here. It was a slim hen

fish with a small, delicate head, and inside it were several eggs still unshed from its last spawning. Unlike the smaller ones, it had the pink flesh which enhanced its popularity on the dinner table. I caught several fish in a short spell and then I reeled in, put the catch on my stringer, and returned to fish the larger loch again at dusk.

Over the hill the wind was falling away and a wide band of water along the far side of the loch was already calm. In the little bay beside the point I could see the widening rings of feeding fish. I removed the hook from my line, replaced it with a little gold Toby, and in the deepening twilight walked over to the point. A few casts there at some distant risers failed to interest a fish. Then, turning to the little bay, I sent the spinner flicking out over the rings of the rising trout to land just short of the rushes at the far side. I retrieved fast just beneath the surface, and halfway back it was taken hard. There was a moment of heavy tension, I tightened, and the line went slack. Another fish rose in the semi-darkness; I cast beyond and it immediately came at the spinner, leapt clear of the water, shook its head, and threw the hook. It was a nice fish but my chance had gone, for only small ones rose now and nothing came again at the spinner.

On the right bank of the loch there is an old stone wall coming down to the water. This wall gives shelter from the westerly winds, and a patch of level turf near the water's edge makes a good camping spot. The ground here was covered with a thick layer of dead grass, of which I pulled up several armfuls, laying them along the ground before putting down my sleeping gear. I then rolled away a boulder next to the wall and prepared the bare space underneath for a fire, removing the dry grass from around it to avoid the risk of flames spreading. My sycamore boughs made poor fuel and it took a long spell of blowing to get the fire burning strongly enough to boil a kettle.

Darkness had brought with it a new sound. A strange whirring echo rose and fell around the loch, its eeriness enhanced by its indefinite source. The sound was produced by the tail feathers of the snipe, a bird I had put up from a sedge patch on my return from the lochan earlier. Other moorland birds often make equally distinctive sounds with their feathers. The short-eared owl, a common daylight hunter in the open hills, will sometimes buzz a human intruder by flying above him and then going into a vertical dive, creating a soft rattling sound with its oddly-angled wings. Like the snipe, this owl will also make its distinctive sound as part of a dusk ritual. The curlew sometimes makes the same sort of manoeuvre towards an intruder as the owl, but its stiffer wing feathers produce a far more startling noise.

There was little wind that night but the sky remained clear and the temperature dropped quickly. The heavy dew which had fallen began to freeze, and after tea I put most of the remaining sycamore on the fire for a last warming blaze. As the weather was dry I had only a light sleeping bag and blanket, and after the fire had died down I buttoned my coat, pulled down my hat, and climbed into the bag. I slept well enough, thanks mainly to the grass mattress, and once again the little space blanket I had carried against emergencies on many such trips remained unopened.

Before falling asleep I heard the far-away song of a skylark. Whether this was the effect of my hearing this song all day, or

whether there was actually a lark singing in the cold darkness, I could not tell. Either way the joyful sound was a welcome accompaniment to the other world.

At dawn I woke to find myself looking at a white wall of mist blending into the frosted ground. The loch had vanished and in its place stood the ibis-form of a curlew. The sun soon broke through and water appeared, shining, calm and marked with the occasional rise. I went to fill the kettle and looked into the clear water. On a previous April visit there had been hundreds of toads here, sitting in motionless pairs across the bed of the loch. This time there were no toads, but above the

water hovered thousands of pale orange flies which set up a loud humming until a gust of wind arrived, at which point the noise stopped as they dropped for cover in the marginal rushes.

I used the last of my fuel to boil the kettle. Then I put out the fire, rolled the boulder back over the fireplace and scattered the grass mattress on which I had slept. The area now looked as it had when I arrived.

Presently a human figure appeared half a mile away on the ridge above the main loch, his silhouette magnified by the skyline perspective. The figure halted at the top of the peregrine rock and sat down, and I knew it was Bill, stopping to look at the view. When he appeared again on the top of the ridge above the boghole I packed up and headed off in that direction.

There is usually some interesting wildlife around this tiny pool. Duck or snipe often rise from it on approach, red grouse cluck from the slope above, and there is frequently a group of mountain hares nearby, their coats at this time of year still showing some winter white. Once, when turning to leave after a fishing spell, a big dog fox jumped from the sedge a yard away and loped off across the hill. Today the only sign of a

predatory creature was the feathered remains of a short-eared owl killed, perhaps, by the same fox.

The wee hole has a trout story of its own. Its surface area is hardly as large as the Cairnsmore lochan, but it is several feet deep and produces a good few pounds of trout a year. Once it had, like the main loch, a limited number of new fish arriving each year from the lochan below. Some grew very large – Alec's father and brother had two- and three-pounders from it, and one-pounders were normal. The first time I cast a line on this miniature pool I hooked and lost one of these big fish, but the next year the outlet stream was cleared to improve drainage on the plateau and this allowed seemingly limitless number of small ones to come up. From that time the hole has held, instead of a few big trout, hundreds of fingerlings. It is, however, a conveniently close source of fish for Alec's re-stocking of the main loch. The eighty-three he had caught from it last year did not seem to have decimated its popula-tion, and a trout took my bait there first cast. Bill came down

the slope and although he was not, supposedly, here to fish, a telescopic spinning rod appeared from his bag and three casts later two more wee trout had left the boghole.

The ridge where Bill had been painting had a fine view of the plateau and its troutwaters. Peaks and ridges appeared on every horizon, some of them showing a suggestion of new green. Here and there a patch of burnt grass showed darkly and a distant haze to the north showed that the shepherds were still at their spring moor-burning.

Our walk back took us nearer the smoking hills. The sun faded to an orange blur as we approached, and the smell of burning grass and heather drifted with the wind. As we passed the derelict cottage four big, brown animals emerged to our right. They looked as large as red deer and were the same dark colour, but the perspective of the hills was again playing its tricks, for they were only hares. A fifth one appeared, nearer and seemingly much smaller, with legs still winter-white.

The fine weather continued for another week. Then, on 23 April, ominous grey cloud swept in on a steady south-easterly wind and by evening a flurry of snow had started. That night and all the next day the snow fell, drifting heavily across the hills. This spring blizzard, more dangerous than its winter predecessors, killed eighty ewes and lambs on the Cairnsmore alone. However, this return to winter was short-lived, for the snow soon started thawing and within days the track to the farm was open again.

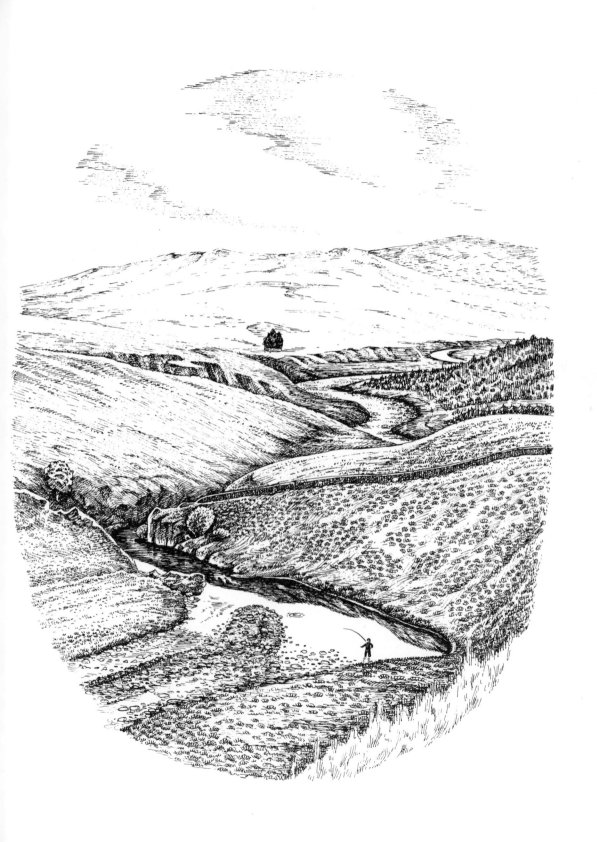

CHAPTER THREE

Summer Patterns

The arrival of the warm season was, in typical northern fashion, accompanied by changeable weather and fresh winds. The first day of May came in with a heavy frost; the following week saw winds from every point of the compass; regular rain showers, some of which fell as snow on the high ground; and even a brief south-easterly gale. Although the trend continued for most of the month, the rough weather could not disguise the signs of summer in the hills.

Areas of light green grass appeared across the face of the big hill behind the farm to join up with the darker green of bilberry patches already showing on the upper slopes. Down below, the sombre mass of conifers was also coming to life as brown bud-casings dropped to the ground by the thousand and yellow-green branch tips burst open throughout the forest. In sheltered places fern and bracken were uncurling and spring flowers added a dimension of fresh colour – primroses, now at their peak on the banks of the Bow Burn, wood anemones along the forest edges, and violets in the moss patches.

Migrant birds continued to arrive, but now they were coming from lands far distant. On the fourth day of May a cuckoo arrived on the lower Bow Burn, a blue-barred male whose call would be repeated throughout the day until he was settled with a mate. On the ninth a pair of swallows came to the farmyard barn; then a small warbler appeared in our garden, one of the late arrivals of the already busy nesting season.

The forest seemed to be attracting new birds by the year as, at the same time, some of the species which were common in its early years were disappearing. Soon after planting, the usual increase in the population of voles attracted big numbers of kestrels, and it was sometimes possible to see several family groups totalling twenty to thirty birds in the air at the same time. Short-eared owls did well too, and on hill walks it was usual to be buzzed by these birds, some of which were attracted from several miles away. After a few years both became scarcer, and now, after twelve years, only a few owls remain along the forest edge, and kestrels have become almost rare. Meanwhile, such typical moorland birds as red grouse and curlew have also left to be replaced by blackcock, an early invader of the young forest, and a whole guide-book of small songbirds. One species which has so far seemed little affected by the changes is the little pipit, a bird which acts as foster-mother to the valley's cuckoos.

The frogs were still spawning loudly during May, but there were other creatures whose regular presence I now missed.

Yellowmouth, the big female adder who lived in a sheltered forest hollow, failed to appear in her sunning spot. Earlier she had spent most of each day lying on the bank in front of a small spruce, usually in the company of her mate, a large slim male with vivid markings, who lived under the next tree. He was out very early this year – I had twice disturbed him lying in the weak sunlight of late January, but he had been too numbed by cold to move away when I approached; yet by early March both snakes were fully active and seemed imper-

vious to the weather. They were out after hard frosts, during
the lashing rains of a south-westerly gale, and even after a
spring blizzard, coiled together on a patch of grass surrounded
by thick snow. There was hardly a day in the month when
they failed to appear.

In early April they were still out regularly, sometimes
together and sometimes under their separate trees; they
became so used to my visits that the sight and sound of my
boots no longer disturbed them. Sometimes Yellowmouth
played a strange sort of game at my approach, running off at
an exaggerated pace around her tree and then immediately
coming back down to lie in front of me again. At the end of
April both snakes failed to appear, and later, when a small
coppery-coloured one took up residence under Yellowmouth's
tree, it began to look as though she had gone for good.

In mid-May the first young trout of the year appeared in the
garden burn. A pair of them came, as they had done in
previous seasons, to our waterhole, tiny creatures hardly
bigger than tadpoles. In the larger pools, now adorned with
fresh leaves of pondweed, there were some larger trout, five or
six inches long, fish which were spending their second and
final summer in the pools before moving down to the Deugh
nearby.

The Water of Deugh rises on Windy Standard, a high
summit just north of the Cairnsmore. Fast, shallow and stony
throughout its fifteen-mile course, the river descends in broad
curves, running west and then south around the main Cairnsmore massif before joining the Ken, its sister river from the
eastern side, in the quiet depths of Ken Doon loch. At the
Green Well of Scotland, the ancient forgotten shrine above the
village of Carsphairn, it is joined by a surfaced road which
follows the final three miles of its course. A part of this road,
the straight section between the Green Well and the village,
has an unrecognized claim to fame, for it was the first road
anywhere with an asphalt surface. The Deugh valley is the
ancestral home of the clan MacAdam, and the MacAdam of
road-building renown chose a convenient place for the experi-
ment which, with the development of the motor vehicle, was
to revolutionize land travel.

At the nearby Holm of Daltallochan, the Deugh meets its
main tributary, the Carsphairn Lane and there, in a typical
location between the two streams, lie the remains of Galloway's remotest stone circle. Below the confluence the Deugh is

a substantial water, but upstream it is only after heavy rain that its broad, boulder-studded course fills out to the proportions of a river. Farther on, the open moors which flank the river come to an end, and the upper half of the Deugh, almost to its source, is enclosed by the new forest.

Our garden pools present a rather different appearance to the nearby middle reaches of the river. The Deugh's swift current does not allow the establishment of pondweed, and the only aquatic vegetation is dark clumps of watermoss, an excellent plant for sheltering water insects, and the yellow-green algae which carpets the stony riverbed. Near our front door a section of drystone wall overlooking a small shallow pool gives convenient cover to a passer-by, and from May onwards I stop here to check on the activities of fish and insect life. By mid-May regular fly hatches have usually begun, and most evenings the surface of the pool is marked by rises or by the bow-waves of trout hunting across the shallows.

The stony bed of this pool shelters a typical variety of the river's aquatic creatures. There are plenty of resident trout up to twelve or thirteen inches long, several shoals of minnows, and good numbers of that odd solitary fish, the stone loach. Apart from the occasional lost rainbow trout from Ken Doon loch, these three are the only species of fish present in the river, as the migratory kinds of other waters nearby – salmon, sea trout and eels – have been prevented access, originally by a natural barrier known as the Tinker's Loup and now by the hydro-dam on the loch.

Around the submerged boulders of this pool can be found those insect types which form a major part of the trout's diet. Stony-cased caddis larvae graze the algal felt, while beneath there are a variety of armour-plated nymphs of the various mayfly types common to the stream and in the fast, shallow runs there are nymphs of a third important type – the stonefly, a creature peculiar to the cold hill-waters. The Greater Stonefly nymph is one of the largest aquatic insects in the river, and its hatching in the month of June marks an important time for the angler. When this stonefly is on the water trout are often encouraged into the sort of active feeding which means success with the artificial fly.

The Greater Stonefly hatch began this year on 29 May. I had stopped by the pool at dusk to see what I took to be a mouse swimming across the middle of it. The current was taking it slowly downstream towards the favoured feeding spot of the largest trout; as the struggling shape neared the centre of the tail of the pool the creature disappeared in a slashing rise. Another dark shape appeared on the surface upstream, and I realized then that I was seeing some of the first adult stoneflies. I got my fly-rod, tied on a very large fly, and returned to the water. Starting from below the pool, I walked up slowly until I was opposite the point where the trout lay. I cast well above it, and when the fly had almost reached the tail I raised the rod and dragged it slowly across the surface towards me. A large bow-wave immediately appeared, but after following for a few feet the trout took fright and shot off towards its lair on the far side.

A few minutes' walk upstream there is another pool, one of the big ones which appear on the river only every mile or so. During the day its placid, hundred-yard length generally fishes poorly, but at this time of year it is the best place for evening visits with the fly-rod. It was from the head of this, the Goose Island pool, that I had caught my first trout of the season on fly.

It had been on a sunny afternoon in early summer, with a warm westerly breeze blowing across the river, as I walked upstream towards the flat expanse of the island. The pair of oystercatchers which nest there had taken off with shrill cries at my approach, circled around, and landed again on the far side. In the main body of the pool ahead only the odd small fish showed at the surface, but in the fast water at the head I spotted a better one rising steadily a couple of feet out from a bankside boulder. I crossed the shallow riffle above the pool and, using the boulder as cover, moved to within a few yards of the fish. It took my small Poacher violently from the surface on the second cast and flew glittering into the air as the hook found a hold. The fish was a handsome one, eleven inches long, in good condition, and brightly marked. Its dominant colours were unusually strong – a classic combination of pale green and orange, common on small fish from certain burn pools but rare in the river. The golden-yellow, a dominant colour on most brown trout, was almost lost in the yellow-green of its upper sides and back as well as in the orange-yellow of its lower fins and tail. A striking feature was the number of bright orange spots along its flanks; I counted over twenty on each.

It is a curious fact that many artificial flies reflect the principal colours of the fish they are supposed to attract. Some of the most successful patterns for brown trout contain dark and often speckled hackles or wings, bodies with a bright touch of yellow or gold, and red or orange tails – typical shades of the fish, and arranged in the same basic positions. The same goes for many traditional sea trout and salmon flies, most of which embody silver plus the brilliant, iridescent colours of these sea-run fish or, in the case of salmon, the orange of its spawning dress. As for Pacific trout, the primary colour of the rainbow – the red of its stripe – is found in many of the classic fly patterns used for both resident and steelhead forms of this fish, while the colours of the cutthroat trout are reflected in the traditional combinations of green, golden yellow, and red. Similarly, the gaudy colours of the Eastern brook trout are found on the bright patterns commonly used for that little char.

This apparent colour mimicry is unlikely to have been a conscious part of the development of these flies, at least in modern times. They were probably created, and certainly long-proven, by what amounts to an exhaustive process of trial and error, and their continued effectiveness seems to point to some simple explanation for their success in different waters and, incidentally, to highlight the trout's acute colour sense.

It is known that the territorial behaviour of trout and salmon results in a lifelong competition between members of the same species, and that over ninety percent of their young can be expected to die as a direct result. The common reaction of a trout to invasion of its territory by a smaller relative is a swift bite to its tail, and a fly which reflects its own colours could well be treated similarly. In the case of a species which is actively feeding in fresh water the fly may more often be taken as a straight food item but, even so, a lookalike effect may improve its chances. To show in practice that a fly has aroused a brown trout's territorial instinct instead of, or as well as, its feeding instinct would be a subtle task indeed, however probable it seems that the territorial element is a likely factor in the success of a lookalike. Negley Farson, in *Going Fishing*, has a description of his most numerous catch of trout, thirty-five fish taken in a river in the Caucasus mountains. The trout had backs of 'a vivid apple green' and in describing their capture he says, 'I . . . discovered that they had a passion for a little orange-and-green-bodied fly, with an inconspicuous wing . . . And when I found out that the trout liked these best I

took off the two other flies and fished with these "United Irelands", as I found out later they were called. It was an unorthodox, bold gesture, but it resulted twice that day in my catching three fish at one time. I have never had more than two on before or since.'

Orange and red, colours infrequently found on natural insects, seem to have a universal appeal to trout, and most traditional wet-fly patterns embody one of these colours. Other proven colours, however, may suggest important characteristics of insects commonly found in the rivers and lochs. The fast-moving nymphs in our window-sill aquarium often catch my eye by a characteristic golden-yellow flash, and the many flies with these colours in the body would be likely to trigger a familiar reaction among hungry trout. On the Deugh,

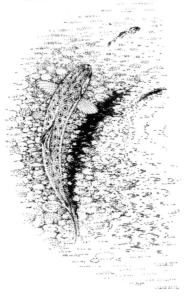

Bill and I have found flies with peacock herl in the body particularly effective; the dark iridescence of this material in such flies as the Coch-y-bondhu represents well the metallic glint of various natural flies and beetles. One fly I am content to use during daylight just about any time of year is the Poacher, with a ginger hackle, peacock herl thorax, yellow body and orange tail.

From mid-May to August the Deugh trout feed actively on small flies throughout much of the day. On warm days of low water, however, they tend to be fussy and, rather than working hard with tiny flies and gossamer leaders for the sake of an odd fish, Bill and I wait for the conditions which make for easy fishing. Typically this will be during a spell of breezy north-westerly weather, when regular showers keep the water fresh and slightly high. On such days the trout take confidently, and a walk along the river with the fly-rod can be productive as well as enjoyable.

A well-fished team of wet flies probably attracts more fish in such conditions than any other method. A downstream wind, however, makes it difficult to cover trout from below and a natural bait, though it may get fewer takes, can sometimes result in more fish hooked and landed. Many common insects will do for bait, but the least troublesome baits to use are those which stay firmly on the hook during casting. Small worms,

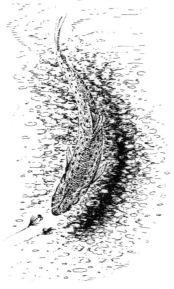

being tough, easily available and much appreciated by the trout, are ideal. In these conditions I fish them downstream, casting into the head of a chosen pool or run from well above it, letting the wind take out a good belly in the line. Fished in this way the bait is easy to control, for it can be guided down the water at any depth while takes can be felt through the belly in the line. Another way with the worm is the upstream method. This has often been described as demanding more skill than any other kind of trout fishing, as it requires both careful stalking and highly accurate casting. A useful tech-

nique in the shallow parts of the river during low water, it is basically the same as the worming method traditionally used on the burns.

A third common style of bait-fishing is the static kind sometimes used on lochs or big riverpools. This, however, tends to be the least effective, for the occasions on which trout will actively hunt around for still objects on the ground are relatively few. The bait is more likely to be taken if it is twitched across the bottom or allowed to drift over it with the current. Another disadvantage of this form of fishing, at least on stony riverpools, is the snagging of the hook under rocks. This can be minimized by remembering never to drag it across the river bed but to assist its course down or across a pool by a series of sharp tugs, leaving the line slack between each. The movement of a bait fished in this way can also be most attractive to feeding trout, and the slacking of the line enables a fish to move off quickly without coming up against the pressure of the rod. A take should, if possible, be followed by a pause to allow the trout to get the hook down before the point is set.

One result of living close by the river is a tendency to fish for brief periods when the trout are feeding well, and most of my fishing is done in the evening within a few minutes' walk of home. The four-hundred-yard stretch from the farm swimming pool up to Goose Island is one of the most varied pieces of water on the middle Deugh, and from May onwards it rarely fails to produce a few fish around sunset. In the larger pools which bound this stretch there is often the chance of a larger trout or two, and when these are dour the shallow runs and pockets will usually give up some smaller ones.

The swimming pool is a small rowan-flanked bowl with an old footbridge linking the high banks above its neck. It is as delightful a place to fish as it is to swim in, and the rocky grottoes which surround its ten-foot depths are as beloved by human divers as they are by the trout which shelter there. At its head is a neat run of white water, and a bait, fly or spinner

OPPOSITE *Summer Trout from the Water of Deugh. From the top:*
12-inch male with typical open river markings
10-inch female from deep, slow lane
12-inch male from fast undercut
9-inch female with many red spots, common on small fish
13-inch male with heavy markings typical of old trout

cast into it at dusk will often be taken by one of the better trout waiting below. The pool is far smaller in area than Goose Island, but it holds plenty of fish up to a pound in weight and occasionally larger.

Above it the river curves away in a steep bend, its fast water dotted with big, bleached boulders. There is one large stone which stands just where the heavier spates throw themselves against the banks of the outer angle of the bend, its face dotted with round cup marks. These strange hollows, which can also be seen on some other big stones along the river, are formed by pebbles catching against them in big spates and grinding around with the force of the water to form anything from a shallow depression to a deep, round cavern with a symmetrical entrance. Above the bend the water opens out into a series of rock-studded pockets, curving back again towards the

TAIL
Gravel deposits comprise main spawning ground, the current flowing through them aerates trout eggs. The broad tail-shallows are also a main feeding area during spates and under cover of darkness.

OVERVIEW

RIVERPOOL: *some features affecting trout*

shallow pool not far from our door. Here there is another chance of a better fish, and during one summer spate Bill took three twelve-inchers here in a quarter-hour spell of fly-fishing. Above this pool is another fast, shallow stretch whose fishable pockets are, like those on most of the river, subject to sudden changes following big floods, particularly those which carry ice-floes during a spring thaw. When a big flood hits the river the booming echoes of dislodged boulders crashing downstream are easily mistaken for the sound of distant thunder.

At the downstream tip of Goose Island there is a big stone which has probably stood through the floods of centuries. Its scoured underside normally shelters a nice trout around twelve inches, and the little run behind it holds several more fish to half a pound or so. Above the boulder the river splits

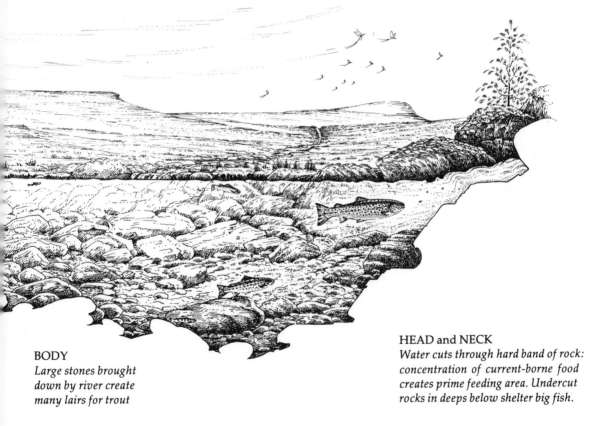

BODY
Large stones brought down by river create many lairs for trout

HEAD and NECK
Water cuts through hard band of rock: concentration of current-borne food creates prime feeding area. Undercut rocks in deeps below shelter big fish.

around the island. The nearside stream is too small to hold anything other than loach and minnows, but the far one has some small runs which hold good numbers of trout. Although the resident fish do not usually exceed nine or ten inches, these runs, like others up and down the river, may sometimes provide a temporary home to larger trout which move about the river during the summer and autumn.

Above, the Goose Island pool itself has a very different character to the shallow reaches of the river. At the top of the pool there is a band of hard rock and over the centuries the water has cut a narrow neck through it. Spates pour through this constricted opening and have cut out a deep channel down the centre of the pool. On either side of this channel there is a long series of undercut boulders which make ideal lairs for the trout. Smaller stones have been swept straight down beyond to form the broad, shallow tail which is an important feeding area as well as the pool's main spawning ground.

Goose Island pool provides more food and better shelter for the larger trout than an equivalent length of shallow, open water. While the population of aquatic insects is probably no greater in a given area than in the fast and shallow stretches, the pool supports big numbers of minnows and loach which, though they compete with the trout in its first year of growth, form an increasingly important part of its diet thereafter. Another important function of the pool is the part it plays during spates when it acts as a settling area for the large amounts of food washed down from bankside and river bed.

As far as the trout are concerned, Goose Island pool is typical enough of its kind, but it is unusually difficult for the angler. Its neck area has been eroded into a series of pockets, which makes it impossible to cover as one entity even in spates and, as the rest of the pool is broad, mostly shallow and very slow, it is awkward to fish it without alarming the trout. Good catches are rare here, even in the most promising conditions. Bill did once hook the pool's big one, only to lose it at the net, and my only notable catch of trout from it came in weather conditions which may not occur again for years. One July there was a week of heavy frosts which killed many plants, including hundreds of young conifers, and it was at dusk on one of these freezing evenings that I took five trout over the half-pound in an hour.

CHAPTER FOUR

Evening and After

A midsummer spell of close and sultry weather put the trout of the Deugh in a strange mood, and the eccentric behaviour of those at Goose Island provided a friend of mine with several entertaining evenings. Towards dusk he would cast a worm into the deepest part of the pool and one of the numerous trout which lie under the boulders would immediately snatch it. It would then run off and if the line were paid out it would often keep going for ten or twenty yards before dropping the bait. When the rod was raised the hook sometimes found a hold for a few seconds, but more often it pulled free immediately and variations on the strike made no difference. The fish kept this up into the twilight and some brief contacts, plus the occasional heavy swirl when one came at the bait on the surface, proved the respectable size of some of them. In fact it seemed to be mostly the larger fish playing this game, running off with the bait in their lips without any intention of swallowing it. If a way could have been found of hooking them a good catch would certainly have resulted, a possibility which kept Louis going, although success escaped him until the mood of the fish changed along with the weather.

During the day the fishing was no better. The trout sipped the occasional mayfly from above their lies but rarely took an artificial with enthusiasm. This situation was an extreme version of one which occurs throughout the season whenever the river remains low, and the only effective answer to it is to fish by night. This was once a popular occupation on the hill waters, though now most anglers stop at darkness when the trout, though still feeding, no longer take small daytime flies and when the fisher, unable to see his world clearly, may sensibly judge his day complete.

In fact, this is the time when a lot of trout, and particularly the big ones, are only just starting to feed seriously and, if the angler can adapt himself to the darkness, his resulting catch may rival that of a good spate. Success at this game requires an approach different from that of daytime for, in the new world of darkness, the waterside environment, behaviour of the fish, and methods of angling take on quite new forms. One great advantage of night-fishing is the cover afforded the angler by the darkness. Stalking is relatively simple, and feeding fish are not easily put off by regular casting. The better trout will usually occupy favourite feeding spots at the head and tail of a pool, and their natural activity at night is complemented by an increased amount of food in the natural drift of the stream including hatching caddis and the big moths which are on the water even on frosty nights in early spring.

Caddis appear early in the season as well, though most seem to be small daylight species. In summer larger kinds are out almost every night, and a lamp usually tempts one or two of them indoors. Textbooks describe these insects as having semi-fossilized mouthparts, a fate which does not seem to prevent some of them joining us for sweetened tea and draining what amounts to several caddis-sized cups. The moths are even greater tea-drinkers, and sometimes one will become quite domesticated, spending the days asleep in some cranny and the evenings filling itself up with the sweet drug until it can no longer move.

My first real success in catching the trout of the Deugh by night came at the close of a warm day one July. I was fishing the tail of a big pool and as darkness fell I sat on a rocky ledge above it and went through my fly tin. The small patterns I had used to catch a couple of eight-inch fish at dusk had had no response from the bigger trout now rising heavily along the hang of the pool, so I looked through an odd assortment of various untried flies, big ones which in daylight would certainly have scared the fish off. First I tried a heavy brown nymph tied on a size-eight hook, casting it towards the tail and retrieving it in fast pulls upstream. Nothing came to it, so I tried another with an orange body and long white wing tied to a long number six. I had a couple of small plucks on this which I missed, but I got the feeling that both this and the first fly were sinking too fast. The next one I chose also had bulky white wings, but it was tied on a lighter, short-shank number-eight hook. I found I could retrieve it just under the surface, and first cast another fish tugged at it but failed to stay on. There was something different in the way these trout were taking the fly compared with the daytime, and the lighter fly now gave me the opportunity to try out a different retrieve.

I cast again, and as the fly neared the tail I began to bring it

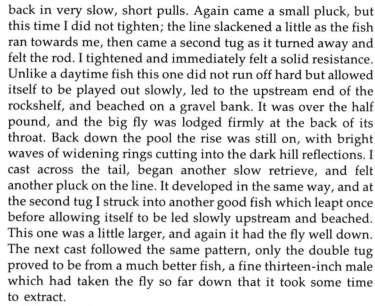

back in very slow, short pulls. Again came a small pluck, but this time I did not tighten; the line slackened a little as the fish ran towards me, then came a second tug as it turned away and felt the rod. I tightened and immediately felt a solid resistance. Unlike a daytime fish this one did not run off hard but allowed itself to be played out slowly, led to the upstream end of the rockshelf, and beached on a gravel bank. It was over the half pound, and the big fly was lodged firmly at the back of its throat. Back down the pool the rise was still on, with bright waves of widening rings cutting into the dark hill reflections. I cast across the tail, began another slow retrieve, and felt another pluck on the line. It developed in the same way, and at the second tug I struck into another good fish which leapt once before allowing itself to be led slowly upstream and beached. This one was a little larger, and again it had the fly well down. The next cast followed the same pattern, only the double tug proved to be from a much better fish, a fine thirteen-inch male which had taken the fly so far down that it took some time to extract.

This forty-five minute spell left me with distinct impressions regarding the night behaviour of the trout. Later attempts confirmed them and I was able to develop further techniques and flies which have proved successful at night from early spring till the end of the season. Tying the new flies was a fairly simple operation, thanks to an experience I had when I discovered the modest skill and equipment needed to create an effective fly. It happened by the banks of a distant stream on the occasion of my wife's first attempt at trout fishing. On arrival I found that my fly tin had been left at home, and while she went up to a likely pool to fish a worm I tried on one of the two flies I had in my lapel. She returned some time later with a good catch, including two half-pounders, and then suggested she try fly-fishing, an idea which was difficult to comply with since I had lost both flies in the bankside alders. Fly-tying materials were in short supply by the water, but on searching the ground round a nearby car park I found two scraps of cloth, yellow and purple, and a piece of tinfoil, which I tied to a hook with a thread from my shirt. Half an hour later my wife, who had never picked up a fly-rod before, hooked and landed a trout on the car park fly. Since then I have no qualms about tying up other, slightly less strange-looking patterns in an equally simple way.

When it came to materials for the night flies I had some help from another family member, my daughter Sarah, who at the age of three developed a remarkable eye for finding small feathers. Where she got them I never found out, but on learning of my new project she presented me with a series of them ideal for the broad flat wing which became the main feature of these flies. A single broad feather an inch or so long, tied on a fine wire, size-eight hook forms the basic pattern. Its lightness allows it to flutter down naturally onto the water and to remain near the surface on a slow retrieve, while the broad wing gives it the necessary surface area when seen from below. Although the creation of these simple flies was based on trial and error, their resemblance in shape and colour to moths and large caddis flies is obvious. A white wing has proved the most constantly successful, and when it does not do well an orange or brown one often will. The uncanny colour-sense of the brown trout seems to operate even on very dark nights.

The first of Sarah's moth-wing flies was an immediate success. One of the feathers she gave me was a small, white, rounded one with a shiny upper side, probably a wing covert of the old gander who scatters his feathers round the farm. Tied on a long-shank, fine wire, size-eight hook, with a body of yellow thread and a small straw-coloured hackle, it looked irresistible and I decided to use it on my first after-dark session of the season.

It was a warm, sultry evening with an intermittent south-easterly breeze and, as dusk deepened on Poacher's Pool, good trout began rising confidently in the centre of the tail. A bat appeared and began to quarter back and forth, competing with the trout for the heavy hatch of night insects. This bat often moves at the fly leader in mid-cast and, in spite of having often tangled his wings in it and letting off a series of loud squeaks, he has not yet lost his interest in it. On this occasion he did not get a chance to tangle himself and the line shot out straight and true towards the ring of the rising fish. The fly fluttered down but it did not reach the water, for just as I was admiring how delicately its white form was descending through the darkness, the water below erupted and it was taken from the air. Almost in the same movement, and before I could strike, the fish was in the air again, tail walking like a wild rainbow trout. It skittered across the pool, splashed back and came out again for what seemed a long time before driving deep and allowing me the reassurance of having it on

Sarah's Moths

55

a tight line. It was well on and I was soon able to steer it upstream to the beaching spot – a half-pound female whose small, delicate head and smooth form veiled the powerful musculature of a brown trout at the peak of condition..

Many other trout have fallen to Sarah's moths since then. The white-winged pattern is perhaps the most consistently effective, but the orange-winged one, based on another of her findings – a small pheasant feather – has proved better on some nights. During the time these simple patterns were evolving I did not have the benefit of any literature on catching brown trout at night from the hill waters, even though I knew that the method had once been widely practised in this area. Then I found a small book, *Trout and how to catch them* by Pat Castle, an expert Borders angler who wrote over fifty years ago on a wide range of trout fishing techniques but whose main practice was to fish by night because 'one gets the best and largest trout at night' and 'It (night fishing) is not nearly such hard work as in day fishing, as one does not need to move about so much – in fact, a couple of good pools is quite enough for a good night's fishing.' He recommends big wet flies dressed flat along the back and fished very slowly. Among other useful night fishing details he mentions the use of the dry fly and a deadly way to fish a maggot; but although he describes ways to fish the big pools, he says little about the shallow stretches in between.

The change which comes over the broad, shallow sections of the Deugh at dusk is remarkable. Large areas which during the day appear to hold nothing but minnows become alive with hunting trout, their wakes disturbing the slick runs and eddies as they swim around in water hardly deep enough to cover their backs. The biggest fish show themselves without their usual caution and a clear evening, when the water surface shines brightly into the twilight, is the best time to spot these fish and to try the difficult job of catching them. Often the larger ones do not show themselves until well into the darkness, and big flies are again needed to attract their attention. If a fly is cast across the area where a hunting trout is seen and, with the rod held high, pulled back across the surface, the fish will often chase it, frequently in a rather leisurely manner ending with a quick nibble or pluck at the fly which rarely results in a good hook hold.

I find a simple answer on the twilight shallows is to fish an unweighted bunch of worms, which the trout will take in the same way as the fly. However, preferring the taste of the worms to a mouthful of feathers, they usually take them down immediately. The bait should be cast a few feet above or beyond a feeding fish to avoid scaring it; if it is not taken at once it can be drawn across the surface in a series of pulls. It can be left to lie for a few seconds between each, for the trout will often follow and take confidently as the bait settles. This method is also deadly after dark at the necks of the big pools, provided the bait is fished near enough to the surface for the fish to spot it.

A serious drawback to summer fishing on the hill waters is the midge which from the latter half of June until early September can become a major problem at dawn and dusk. The usual insect repellants will temporarily stop midges biting face and hands, but when out in numbers they will not be discouraged from swarming over exposed places, getting into eyes and finding their way into biteable spots beneath collars, cuffs and socks, quickly turning the fishing – particularly fly-fishing – into a refined form of torture. At these times even an insect net or stocking on the head will extend fishing time only briefly, as their swarms soon build up to unchallengeable proportions. After dark they normally retreat to the ground again, the lack of midges being another advantage of night fishing. Excessively warm and sultry weather conditions, however, sometimes encourage them to remain active into the darkness. In July this year I fished on three such difficult nights consecutively.

On the first occasion I went out at dusk. The midges immediately closed in as I put up the tackle, but they were not out in full force and, in spite of their attention, I was quickly able to get a big white-winged moth out across the tail of a pool. I caught a fish at once, a little under the half-pound, and followed it with a smaller one before missing several better trout which snapped at the fly but refused to take it down with their usual confidence. At one point one of the rare Deugh big ones rose heavily under my bank a couple of rod lengths downstream. I cast over it, and the fly landed at the centre of the rise; the big fish came up immediately but missed it. I pulled the line back gently and re-cast it in the same movement, but the wary monster now refused to be tempted, and as it was now a little after midnight – the time when the trout start their usual two-hour break – I packed up.

On the second evening I walked up to Goose Island. The day

had been particularly hot and close and a thick cloud layer held the heat in at night. Not a single trout rose in the dusk, and the water was so warm that it must have been approaching a dangerous temperature for them. That night the midges swarmed in vast numbers and serious fishing would have been impossible even if the trout had been hungry.

The third day dawned again with unabated heat. An intermittent southerly breeze did little to clear the sultry air, but early in the afternoon a light, steady rain started. It did not herald a real change in the weather, which was to continue for several midge-laden days, but it brought a welcome change in the atmosphere and put the river up by an inch or so. I was hopeful that fresh water would put the trout back in form and I set off early, intending to fish the evening rise in some of the smaller pools as darkness fell.

The rain had now stopped, and the pungent smell of wet vegetation brought a welcome change to the heavy air. Fish had not yet begun to stir in the small runs which I passed, moving quickly across the grassy tussocks which flank the course of the stream. Halfway down, where the Deugh makes a wide turn, I startled a feeding roe deer in its orange summer dress which bounded off a few yards into the nearby conifers, stopped, turned, and barked at me. I barked back and the animal sprang off into the forest with graceful bounds. I went on down the final straight stretch of river, across the stony delta of a small burn and on to a small pool tucked against a jutting granite overhang. Intending to fish a bait in the last of the light, I stopped here to put up the long cane fly-rod and attach a reel loaded with six-pound nylon.

I walked in against the edge of the overhang and put a small worm on the hook. The rain had started again and, between intermittent gusts of warm wind, clouds of midges began their onslaught. Conditions were rapidly becoming inauspicious, but although I had not yet seen a trout rise my worm was snatched by one on the first cast into the top of the pool. I struck but missed, and when the same thing happened on the next cast it seemed as though the fish were in a game-playing mood and were not after all responding to the fresh water. The third cast, however, made contact and a nine-incher left the river, the deeply set hook proving the serious intent of its take. I soon caught two smaller fish and, in the deepening twilight, I decided to move on to the larger Midpool.

The Midpool has all the qualities for angling which Goose

Island lacks. It is a neat oval bowl easily fished from one spot; the big boulders which line its deep centre shelter plenty of trout but rarely snag the hook. Its only real drawbacks are the high banks which bound it on both sides and make an unobserved day-time approach difficult. In the twilight, however, this was no longer a problem and I quickly climbed down to a strip of stones a rods length away from where the fast water of the narrow neck meets the deeps below.

I flicked the bait into the neck, followed down with the rod as the current took it into deep water, and felt the fast tug of a fish. I slackened the line momentarily, struck, and hauled out a quarter-pounder. I put another worm on the hook, more now by touch than by sight, and caught another the same size. On the next cast a better trout immediately took it in the fast water under the rod-tip, a half-pounder on whose flanks I could still make out its unusually large spots. On the next try the worm was intercepted again a few feet downstream by another good trout – an eleven-incher – which was quickly joined by one more a little larger yet. As the light went, the better trout were obviously concentrating at the neck of the pool.

The next cast fished down without interception, but on the retrieve I felt the line catch against a troublesome boulder which lies deep down the neck. I pulled hard, slackened, and pulled again, hoping that a fish, as sometimes happens, had taken the line round the boulder and was still on, but the inflexibility of the tackle told me I was well snagged. I tugged again and this time had the impression that the weight, though no less inflexible, had shifted position. Something as solid as a rock but which somehow was not a rock, began to move: I then realized that, in those magic moments between day and night, I had achieved the rare honour of becoming attached to that singular creature, the biggest trout in the pool. The fish suddenly shot downstream and thirty yards away, between the cliff portals of the tail, leapt high into the air, a dark shape against the sky reflections. I had too little line on my reel for a trout of this kind and I was already at the end of it; the fish jumped a second time, and I had started to follow it downstream when the line fell slack. The fish was now running towards me so I reeled in quickly to make contact again in the deep water nearby. Off it ran again, though hardly fifteen yards this time, and under heavy pressure came back and began to make shorter head-shaking runs along the left bank. When it seemed safe to hold it hard, I bent down at

the waterside and with one hand cleared the stones away from a small area to create a safe beaching place. I splashed water across it, then in one smooth movement drew the heavy fish up the shingle. Sixteen inches plus of prime wild trout suddenly lay kicking at the base of the cliff, six feet from the water's edge. I grabbed its broad back with both hands and, with blessings for the future, turned it over and brought its head down hard on a sharp-edged stone. The darkness did not prevent appreciation of the magnificent physique of the fish, a sharp-snouted male in top condition and approaching two pounds in weight.

In spite of midges and weather my total catch had turned out to be a good one: eleven fish, weighing altogether over five pounds, in seventy-five minutes. I had one more cast, and when a fingerling grabbed the worm I took it as a sign to pack up and leave.

The night walk home from here is a familiar affair, though not without its hazards. A slip on the steep bank above the Midpool could mean a fall of thirty feet, and a succession of treacherous, meandering sheep-paths, bog patches, unexpected boulders and the hidden gulleys of small watercourses make the rest of the walk a potential obstacle course for anyone unfamiliar with crossing rough ground by night. To move quickly and safely requires concentration, not only to make use of what light there is but also to centre one's own thoughts which, lacking the familiar stimulation of the daylight visual world, easily slip into a state of imagination more troublesome than any external hazards.

Groups of night anglers commonly display loud and fearful behaviour on the river bank after dark, but the solitary fisher cannot afford the luxury of such reactions. Having no other human presence to reassure him, he is obliged to accept the darkness so completely that he becomes a part of it and can move around with confidence. He has to face a whole new world of sound: of disturbing night noises, shufflings and bumps, unaccountable whirrings and gratings made by night creatures he may never see. He has to accept with equanimity the not uncommon occurrence of sensing things which will not fit into his rationale, nor perhaps anyone else's. At night there is no dividing line between the sensations brought to him by his heightened hearing and other subtler effects, often associated with particular places, whose solidity he cannot confirm and which may have more in common with dreams than the everyday world.

If he cannot accept the conditions of darkness the angler may as well stay at home because he will make a poor night fisher and a dangerous companion. But if he can adapt, he should quickly find himself enjoying the fishing and even the strange effects of his only half-solid nightworld. He will learn to move with speed and confidence over strange ground on moonless nights, and to trust his feelings as well as his eyes. He will still need to watch his reactions carefully, for should he find himself stumbling around on leaving the water he will need to slow down immediately and concentrate his energies before carelessness leads to a fall.

He will also need to be constantly prepared for strange encounters, not all of them of an insubstantial kind. The remarkable creatures of the night will need to be accepted for what they are rather than for what they represent, since alarm is an unnecessary reaction to the flitting bat as he flies against the line, the soft-winged and curious owl, or the big moths which sometimes land on the quiet form of the angler. Alarming encounters can be expected with other kinds of creatures; one of the commonest is the nightmarish appearance of a huge, white, irregularly shaped form directly ahead of the night walker which suddenly turns into the white markings of a cow, hardly a classic creature of the night. Often the quiet walker will come across wild creatures less efficient than he in moving in the dark; the clumsy crashes of a deer or the wild flutterings of a startled bird, tangled in the branches of its own roost, may convince him of his place among the hunters of the night. It is a role he affirms each time he returns with a good catch of fish. The experienced angler can become one of the deadliest of night hunters, and he is rarely likely to meet another creature whose abilities in the dark rival his own.

One night last summer I came across such a creature. I had gone up to Goose Island at twilight to try for a big trout whose feeding routine I had watched for several previous evenings; on approaching the tail of the pool I saw a big rise which, although rather farther up than I had seen it before, looked like the same fish. I shifted a few yards up the bank when a dark shape moved across the sky-reflection of the upper pool. I sat down to watch, disappointed that a mink, the unpopular water weasel which has appeared in recent years in the hills, should disturb my fishing. The moving shape, however, looked rather bulky, less like a swimming mink than the head of a larger animal, and when it went under I was left wondering if there could be an otter in the pool. My question was answered a minute or so later when a large beast shot up out of the water just below me with a great snort. An otter had once before done this to me in a remote loch, a place where they were normally abroad all day and had not acquired the nocturnal habits of other otters. That afternoon an otter's head had reared from the water hardly two feet away from mine, and both parties had fallen backwards onto, or into, their respective elements. This time, however, it was dark and the animal did not seem to recognize me, although it remained above water for some time watching the glow of my cigarette. It seemed ironic that on the only occasion I went out specifically to try for a big trout I should meet a rival more likely to catch it than all the rest of its predators combined.

This year the otter was at Goose Island again, and on three successive outings it swam under the rod as I fished the head of the pool at twilight. Each time it appeared again farther down the pool, disturbing the water with great waves and coming up to watch me from different spots. Its appearance did not distract me from fishing, though it disturbed the trout for a short time after its passing, and my lack of interest in it may have prompted the strange happenings which took place later on the third night.

I had left the head of the pool, having caught a trout there after the otter's passing, and was approaching the tail when the animal appeared again from under the bank a few feet ahead. It dived and swam across the shallows, raising a great bow-wave as it went, and after watching me briefly from a rock on the far side, it swam, to my surprise, straight back towards me. I knelt down by the water, and the next moment it erupted an arm's-length away. It dived again but this time

remained under the near bank a few yards upstream, and I continued on my way, intending to catch another trout or two down towards the swimming pool.

A few minutes later I was casting my fly across a small run at the bottom of Bill's garden when the otter suddenly surged under the rod. I then realized that the creature, which had presumably followed me downstream, was trying to play with me. In its boldness, however, it had given the advantage in the game to me, and I raced to the end of the run to turn the animal back. We reached it at the same moment, and the otter turned in a great swirl to swim upstream again. I overtook it, and then a strenuous game ensued as I ran back and forth to prevent it from leaving the run. There would be a regular pause as the beast came up for air with a great snort beside a particular bankside boulder only to find me looking it in the face, and then the action began again, though after a while we both became rather out of breath and our mutual admiration sessions by the boulder became longer. Although it had not tried to get away across the river I was not sure that my game was not proving a little more than the otter had reckoned on, and I eventually left it in peace.

Since the regular appearance of otters I have had less expectation of a big trout from the pools around the farm, but I was pleased to have taken a fourteen-incher, the largest to date from the swimming pool, only days before that encounter. Since then I have had opportunities to get to know the animal better, but having once had the dubious pleasure of living with an otter I decided to encourage it no further.

CHAPTER FIVE

Diversions

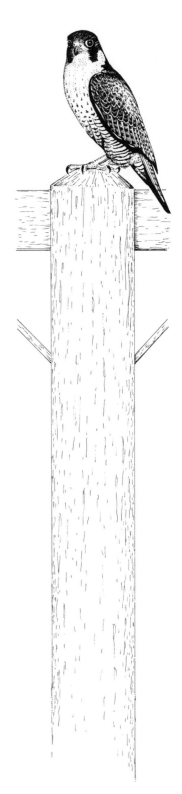

The summer turned into one of those which occur every now and again to disprove the stereotyped image of Scottish weather. Throughout July the land basked in the steady heat of the sun, and as hot days became weeks, broken only by the odd thundery shower, it seemed as if this sort of summer was quite the normal thing here. Fortunately for the farmers, the weather held over the risky haymaking period and, just as fortunately, there had been enough rain earlier in the season to water the land when it needed it most. Apart from anglers, for whom the weather is almost never right, the only real complaints about the hot spell concerned the record-breaking numbers of midges.

Other insects seemed to thrive in the heat too. Wasps and big bumble-bees were unusually numerous, and the forest hummed with flies. Along the fringe of the trees an exotic procession of birds passed by, a few of them stopping to look in at the windows of my caravan studio. Some of the young birds were rash enough to try to come inside, and although only one of them, a young swallow, succeeded, the parents of warblers, bullfinches, wheatears and reed-buntings hovered nervously around as their offspring fluttered against the windows. A larger species also took an interest in the goings-on around the farm this year, a pair of peregrine falcons having settled in the area following – perhaps significantly – an increase in the number of wood pigeons in the forest. The older peregrines became quite curious about the humans, and one appeared almost daily, flying low across the farm. One day, as I left the caravan after a spell of writing, the brown-backed younger bird swished over my head as I opened the door and landed on a nearby telegraph pole. It sat there for a long time watching as several people walked back and forth below, glancing down with baleful curiosity whenever some-one stopped to look up at it. Both birds hunted around the farm and one day in June the older one, chasing a small bird, drove its prey against our kitchen wall with a loud thump.

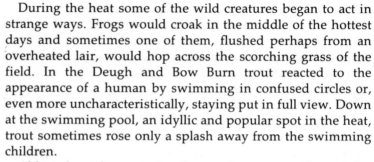

During the heat some of the wild creatures began to act in strange ways. Frogs would croak in the middle of the hottest days and sometimes one of them, flushed perhaps from an overheated lair, would hop across the scorching grass of the field. In the Deugh and Bow Burn trout reacted to the appearance of a human by swimming in confused circles or, even more uncharacteristically, staying put in full view. Down at the swimming pool, an idyllic and popular spot in the heat, trout sometimes rose only a splash away from the swimming children.

Although angling was hardly a serious proposition on the river in day time, the dry weather did not stop a few catches being made in other places. The summer hills now had an added attraction, as their broad faces, softened by flower-studded swards, are never far from the watery enchantments of the high glens where summer visitors may discover the delights of the forgotten hill burns.

The number of such burns in any part of Scotland is, from the viewpoint of the individual angler, practically infinite. In our valley the largest of them is the Bow Burn, and the shady depths of the Black Glen are within easy reach for summer walks, picnics, fishing and bilberry-picking trips. A variety of other small burns, each with its distinctive charm and character, join the Deugh throughout its course. The Polsue, which runs into the river not far downstream, is one of the most substantial, although it can be jumped or waded almost anywhere down its two-mile length except after heavy rain, when it pours off the Cairnsmore in a respectable torrent. Until this year I had regularly crossed the delta of this burn, and even placed stepping stones there for use during spates, without exploring beyond the first few bends. This spring I got to know it better through Bill's dyking project which took place on the Black Shoulder not far from the source.

By midsummer Bill and his partner had completed a mile of wall, and I was going up to the Black Shoulder regularly with a neighbour from the valley. Jim and I had undertaken to dig out the sunken remains of the old dyke ahead of the builders, and once a week we would cross the middle reaches of the Polsue and climb the ridge beyond in order to spend the day grappling with an unending assortment of glacial boulders, an archetypal sort of occupation which contrasted sharply with the vast and ever-changing panoramas dropping away below us.

We were working steadily towards the little barren lochan which sits at the base of the shoulder. Whenever the wind died away its silver disc shone smooth and serene; not a rise disturbed it, and the closer it got the more fishless it appeared. At the end of the month, when we were nearing the closest point between wall and lochan, it was decided to remedy the situation with the help of the Polsue burn trout.

On our next visit we set off early, up through the band of forest behind the farm and onto the final stretch of a rough track which runs along the lower slope of Dodd Hill. There is a cut-away bank above the track which is covered by lush multicoloured mosses at this time of year and dotted in places with two kinds of insectivorous plants – the red-stemmed lesser sundew on the flat wet areas along the base of the bank and the butterwort on more watered parts of the slope.

At the end of the track we cut down through the conifers to our usual crossing-place on the Polsue and stopped to put up some tackle. We fished upstream, keeping low, and in every run and glide wee trout snatched and wrestled the worm. We stopped only to transfer each fish from hook to water-filled plastic bag, and very soon seven fingerling trout were swimming around inside.

The last part of our route consisted of a mile-long diagonal climb to the ridge nearly a thousand feet above the burn, and for the sake of the fish we moved fast. Our pace helped aerate the bag, and since the trout showed no distress in transit there was no need to look for a change of water. They arrived at the lochan looking less tired than we did, and as the temperature of the water there matched that in the bag the little fish were released gently straight into their new home.

Infant trout, like the young of other creatures, are less prone than adults to shock as a result of fast environmental changes. We were not, however, prepared for the next move on the part of our fish; within minutes of their introduction, several began busily eating insects on the surface of the lochan. We watched the widening rise-rings, conscious that they were likely the first ever to appear there. Whether the trout would survive a hard winter in the shallow water was open to question, but provided that the big heron which sometimes flies over the shoulder did not bother them, or a heavy storm blow all the water away, they should spend at least one summer happily depleting the lochan's natural food supply. From the angler's point of view it might be preferable if only a

couple were to survive, as the food should be sufficient for these to grow quickly to a good size, and thereby provide incentive for the good walk necessary to reach their hilltop home.

We went over to the new wall and sat down on the lee side for tea before starting work. On previous visits there had often been new features appearing in the landscape as we watched, and today was no exception as the changing light produced a kaleidoscope of shifting effects among the mountains to the west. On clear days some very distant features came into view – the soft blue smudges of mountain ranges seventy miles away and more appearing on distant horizons. To the north-west, beyond Loch Doon and the Ayrshire hills, the sharp peaks of Arran and the Western Highlands fade westwards to the Mull of Kintyre and, beyond that again, the far peaks of Jura and Islay. On the south-western horizon, beyond the Rhinns and a stretch of ocean, appear the Mountains of Mourne in Ireland; while to the south, out over the shining waters of the Solway Firth, stands the Isle of Man. England, too, can be made out to the south-east, where the Lake District fells raise their distinctive forms.

Except on days when the cloud is low the most dramatic views are relatively near. Beyond the Deugh valley runs the north-south chain of the Rhinns of Kells and these, together with the Merrick range beyond, comprise one of the most remote and rugged pieces of terrain in Scotland. During the last Ice Age this area was, after Rannoch Moor, the largest centre of glaciation, and like that renowned moor it has a long history as a place of wilderness refuge. Such famous figures as Robert the Bruce and Robert Burns have become part of the tradition of the area. The Covenanters hid in its hills, living in desperate conditions before their ill-fated march towards Edinburgh, while an older story tells of a family of cannibals who once lived on its fringes. S. R. Crockett, the author of romantic Galloway novels, pictures them waylaying travellers and disposing of their remains in a dark corner of Loch Neldricken, still marked on the map as the Murder Hole.

Today the moor still continues its traditions of wilderness. Hill-walkers come here regularly from the cities and towns, and although gates on the new forest roads now limit motor access, there are still some splendid hiking routes along the chain of the Rhinns and across the dramatic wastes between the Rhinns and the Merrick. This is excellent fishing country, although in some places anglers are supposed now to pay for their sport, and the fishing in some of the lochs has suffered in recent years from the scourge of acid rain. Most of the area has, under the auspices of the Forestry Commission, been turned into a National Forest Park; the few permanent habitations are no more, and the dramatic desolation of the central moor has been enclosed by great tracts of conifers. The coming of the Forest Park, however, has failed to protect the area from a scheme which, if it should go ahead, would rival the more sinister events of the past.

There is a mountain in the central moor, known for its striking rock formations and its role as the home of a pair of Galloway's few remaining golden eagles. The proposed scheme specifies the insertion into the granite heart of this mountain containers of the most poisonous substance known: plutonium, in the form of nuclear waste. Should the plan go ahead it is not only the eagles which will be lost, but everything which these birds represent to the people who come here. The historic continuity of the moor as a place of wilderness refuge would be permanently shattered by the corruption of the Mulwharchar at its centre.

The Mulwharchar drains into Loch Doon, the largest still-water in the south of Scotland, which lies towards the north end of the moor. The last owner of this loch bequeathed it to the public as a free angling water; it is a popular one, though never crowded, for the road which serves it gives access only to a fraction of its twenty-odd miles of shoreline. Until recently its fish population consisted of large numbers of smallish brown trout and char with some seasonal sea trout and salmon, but over the past few years there have been dramatic changes, first in an increase in the size of the brown trout, and then in the appearance of the perch which now patrol the shoreline in droves.

The char fishing in Loch Doon has long been regarded as some of the best in Britain, for unlike those from other large char waters these fish can be caught all season on fly from the shore. Exquisitely coloured, they average nine or ten inches and occasionally reach a pound in weight. Since their isolation in the loch after the retreat of the glaciers the arctic char here, like those of other relict populations, have undergone some remarkable physical changes, developing the narrow tailstalks and swallow-tails of free-swimming shoalfish as well as the small mouths of plankton-feeders. The tiny crustaceans on

71

which they mainly feed tinges their rich flesh a bright orange, and local people have always regarded char as delicacies. The only complaint to be heard about these delightful fish is that their shoals usually pass by too fast and too infrequently to allow an angler to take enough for a good meal.

Out of the fringes of the moor, or from the virtually continuous Cairnsmore range, spring many burns, including the headwaters of all the major rivers of south-west Scotland: Doon to the north, Girvan and Stinchar to the west, Nith to the east, and Dee to the South. The Deugh is at the upper end of the Dee system and after joining the Ken it runs down to Loch Ken ten miles to the south. Here it meets the Black Water of Dee and then, as the plain Water of Dee, continues south from Loch Ken for another ten miles or so to the Solway Firth.

The views from the Black Shoulder provided visual entertainment during our tea-breaks, but there were occasional sound effects too. One of these, the sound of waterfalls, occurred when the wind blew from the direction of the big slope above the source of the Polsue burn. Its face was smooth and unmarked save for boulder outcrops higher up, and the source of the sound remained a mystery until I went over towards it one evening after work.

The place was at about the same elevation as the shoulder, and as I walked across the intervening hillside the sound of falling water became louder. There was still no sign of a burn, and it was not until the sound came from right under me that its source became apparent. The smooth turf slope was in fact only a skin across the surface of a great glacial boulder-field, and the sounds, issuing from hidden shafts, were the magnified noises of underground streams crashing down through caverns below. They came from across a broad area, but at the base of the slope became concentrated as the rivulets found a common course,. and then the young Polsue burst forth, a waterfall from a bouldery cavern.

Below it was a series of other small waterfalls, then the tiny burn ran fast and narrow across more even ground. Here I saw the first trout, a pair of fingerlings at the tail of a wee run, lying close together just as they do in our waterhole. By the end of the year these two fish would doubtless be losing their neighbourliness and taking up territories downstream, somewhere below the nearby confluence with the tiny tributary dropping down from the lochan. Below it there were larger fish, six- and seven-inchers which darted under stones or

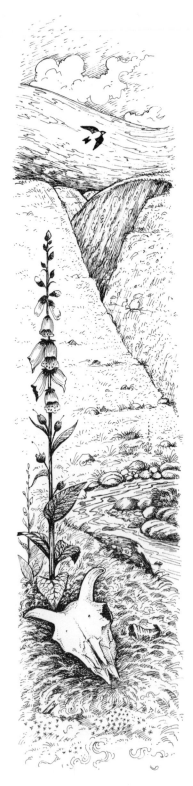

panicked back and forth across little pools as I came upon them.

Further on the burn cut down into a steep gulley and here were more waterfalls. Some, with ten- and fifteen-foot drops, had scoured out deep holes among the large boulders which lay across the gulley floor, and I wondered whether the trout above the falls had been planted by man or had been living there since before the waterfalls were formed, or whether they had crawled up around them during the autumn spates. The delectable pools below had me imagining half-pounders and I decided to return here with a rod.

On a hot day the following week I set off up the burn with Jim to fish and take photographs. We walked up to the crossing-place and, turning upstream, picked our way between stream-side boulders and the eroded banks of the high gulley. Its steep sides, graced by stately foxgloves, were green with summer, and at every twist of the burn there was some small surprise. Near the crossing-place we came upon the carcass of a ewe, a victim of the April blizzard, and farther on another. Wagtails flew back and forth across the burn, catching flies in the warm afternoon air, and fat dippers rose from it to fly low upstream with piercing calls. A pair of white-rumped sand martins started up from the gravel face left by a collapsed bank, and over the Black Shoulder a buzzard appeared, soaring on high currents.

Bird-watching stopped as we reached the first of the pools. The water fell seven or eight feet over a projecting lip of rock, creating a pool of almost equal depth below. Beside the fall a small, bushy willow clung to the rockface, just out of the grazing range of a blackface sheep, and as we watched a trout rose beneath it.

I moved up from below and prepared for the first cast. The small worm arched across the water, bounced off the waterfall and was sucked into the depths beneath. Then came a fast double tug; I struck, and an eight-inch trout leapt against the rod – a good enough fish for a tiny burn, but half the size I was hoping for. Next cast produced a seven-incher, and we moved upstream. Every little pool seemed more delightful than the last, and with a cautious approach from below, each of them gave up its trout. I soon had a dozen, though the largest was under nine inches and I had to conclude that the pools, though spacious enough for bigger fish, could not provide the food for their growth.

In places the banks of the Polsue opened out to create small, boulder-studded terraces on either side. On some of them the stones looked like the half-buried remains of ancient castles, the bases of walls and portals still discernible, though most had been created by the action of ice and water. One, however, was the work of man, a small one-room bothy, rectangular in outline with the fireplace still recognizable. The inhabitant of this forgotten place must have had a fine view down several miles of open slopes to the distant village of Cairsphairn.

I had seen the lower part of the Polsue mostly from a distance, but it was obvious that there were no more large pools along it. I had crossed it a couple of times when helping my neighbour Simon to bring a bull to the farm from a distant hillside to visit his cows. The first time the bull had proved to be well enough behaved but to have had no head for heights. On approaching the Polsue gulley it had pushed on straight over the lip, sat back on its haunches and began to slide down the steep slope. It descended fast, leaving a trail of broken turf in its wake, hit the bottom with an earth-shaking thump, rolled forward onto its feet and continued on its way.

Although its trout are small, the Polsue, like other small streams, has advantages. Big catches can be taken in weather conditions unsuitable for fishing larger waters; the trout are also easy to catch, which makes it a good place for beginners. It is further away than the Bow Burn, but when four of the younger children at the farm wanted to go fishing this year, it was to the lower Polsue they went for their first try.

The party set off downriver on a windy afternoon towards the end of June. On reaching the Polsue confluence we turned up into the sheltered glen of the small burn and prepared the tackle: a light nine-foot pole and an equal length of six-pound line armed with a size-fourteen hook. Then, after demonstrating the baiting of the hook with a small worm, I suggested that I guide each child in turn while the rest watched, or did not watch, from a distance.

With Sarah, the youngest, I went a little way upstream and crept to the lip of a bank above a small run. Then, flipping the worm upstream, I gave her the rod and waited for it to drift into a deep spot directly below us. We waited only briefly before the rod jagged sharply: a pause, and I said, 'Pull it up!' Then ensued a good struggle as Sarah hauled on the long rod which leapt in her hands as the trout, a large enough fish for a

75

four-year-old, lashed on the end. She looked in awe as it eventually came up over the bank, and I helped her unhook the heavily spotted trout, bang it on the head, and string it through gills and mouth with a piece of sedge grass. She ran downstream to show it to her mother while I rebaited the hook for the next angler.

Becka, at seven years old, already had some fishing experience, having had some success at catching minnows in a tea-strainer on the Deugh. A hundred yards or so upstream a large boulder rose from the burn and, suspecting a likely pocket of water below it, I walked up with her away from the water's edge until we were above the spot. Then, after crossing a riffle, we went downstream again, keeping the big boulder between us and the suspected pocket. We crouched down behind the stone and I showed Becka how to guide the bait into the fast water beside us and, keeping the rod-tip low, to let it drift down out of sight behind the big stone. Then the unexpected happened: instead of throbbing to the tugs of a seven-incher, the rod jagged down sharply to the pull of a good fish. I leapt aside to give Becka room to stand and play it. She handled it instinctively, putting a fine bend in the rod as a half-pound trout leapt and splashed in the open water beyond its bouldery lair. Within two or three minutes she had it out, and a new Polsue record lay thumping its tail on the bankside grass.

It was then the turn of Becka's nine-year-old sister to try her luck. The next pool was long and narrow with a convenient stone near the tail which gave cover from below. The worm flew upstream and was taken as it hit the water by a seven-incher covered in bright red spots. Marcia quickly got the hang of the game, and a couple of weeks later she caught a half-pounder unaided during a rising spate at the head of the Goose Island pool of the Deugh.

Lastly came the turn of Chun, the only man in the party. His pool was a short, fast one with a waterfall at the head; we circled around it, came in low by some large stones above, and let the fall take the worm down to the fish. Once again it was taken without hesitation; Chun, drawing himself up to his six-year-old height, stood proudly above the fall and, with a look of great satisfaction, hauled in his first fish.

By now we had wandered far upstream and it was already time to leave. The party set off well satisfied and were soon at the Deugh confluence regaling astonished mothers with tales of piscatorial exploits. I took the opportunity to try for a trout of my own from the river. Within minutes I had one which was, to the delight of the children, a mere six inches long, the smallest of the day.

Most of the children who have caught a first trout from the Polsue have done so without any prior knowledge of angling. One of them, however, had been hooked on fishing long before he had hooked a fish. At eight years of age, Tom was already an armchair expert – he even tied his own flies – and his capture of a seven-inch Polsue burn trout was the culmination of a year spent in perusing fishing literature and accumulating tackle. His enthusiasm brought its rewards when he ended a week's fishing in hot and difficult weather with a nice catch from the Deugh, including his first half-pounder.

One of the pleasures in fishing with children, apart from their enthusiasm, is the unexpected events which occur. Becka's half-pound trout was not the only large one to have been taken on such a trip; the first half-pounder I saw from the Bow Burn was caught by a visiting boy in a similar way.

Fishing with adults seems to be less predictable. Experienced anglers usually follow their personal routines, although some who have fished only large, open waters show a remarkable lack of insight into the wild trout's behaviour. Adult beginners often seem slower than children to catch on to the basics of fishing due, perhaps, to a loss of instinctive curiosity about what goes on under the water.

One adult who had no such limitations was Richard, Bill's dyking partner on the Cairnsmore wall. He had listened to fishing stories from me and Bill with unusual interest, and soon after acquired a short fibreglass rod and fixed-spool reel on which he caught a small trout from the burn in front of his house. This burn, which runs through low rolling hills into Loch Ken, has an even smaller flow than the Polsue, but the rock over which it runs has given it some special features. There is a series of deep, lily-studded pools which allow trout weighing up to a pound to survive even during dry spells when the burn itself virtually dries up. There are lanes, too, long canal-like sections where the trout grow even larger. Richard had caught his first fish from a lane, and soon after decided to try fly-fishing there. He tied a piece of crow feather around a big hook, put it on the end of his nylon line, and let his apparition drift over the lane in a stiff wind; it was still a foot or so above the water when a thirteen-inch trout leapt out,

grabbed the fly and was successfully landed. Last year, fishing a worm at the top of this lane in a summer spate, still with his original tackle, he took an eighteen-inch, two-and-a-quarter pounder.

The Polsue holds no such monsters; its charms are rather those of a fast headwater stream. Before I arrived it had probably not been fished for years, but like many small waters

Dwarf Birch

Scottish Grey Birch

Silver Birch
Wild Birch Leaves: Actual size

it had been capable of producing at least one half-pound trout as well as plenty of pan-sized ones. The worth of such streams lies not only in their beauty but also in the high food value and easy exploitation of the numerous trout they contain. Burn-fishing, unlike that of larger waters, relies hardly at all on weather conditions, and it is usually possible to catch at least eight or ten trout an hour. A hard-working angler with the right tackle should be able to catch several dozen trout a day almost anytime between April and October, although it is advisable to avoid streams which constitute natural nurseries for heavily-fished waters, or those which contain the young of sea trout and salmon. Not long ago burns regularly provided an important addition to family meals, and an old man I know remembers his father returning home with twelve dozen trout from a Saturday's burn-fishing, enough to provide his eight children with several good breakfasts in the coming week. Burns fished in this way may be expected to suffer easily from over-fishing, but often the reverse is true, for their natural productivity is so great that such catches, if made annually, can lead to an increase in the average size of the trout – an added attraction for the angler. It is a widely held belief in Scotland that the hill burns which are still fished regularly tend to produce better trout than the neglected kind.

When out for a big burn catch I find the usual rod-and-reel too clumsy. Continuous long casting is unnecessary and wastes time, the advantage of distance being outweighed by the manoeuverability of a light ten-foot wand, a fixed ten or ten-and-a-half feet of nylon, and a scrap of lead shot a foot or so above a size-fourteen hook.

With this outfit it is possible to walk upstream behind the fish, keeping low and flicking the line ahead with an unobtrusive sideways swing. The bait can be sent very accurately up to twenty feet into the heads or tails of pools, or into small pockets, without alarming the trout, and the hard work which this boulder-hopping method entails is compensated for by the weight of the catch. A deadly lure is a small artificial fly with the barb removed to facilitate quick unhooking.

CHAPTER SIX

High Water

It was August before the rains finally arrived. The Deugh had lain low for weeks, and some success in night fishing had not made up for the lack of big river catches which can be made in a good spate. The long-awaited high water, washing food from the banks of every watercourse in the hills, put the trout into a frenzy of feeding and made it possible to even the score with fish in the more difficult pool where the most inexperienced fisher could now expect a catch.

Since the planting of the forest it had taken only a couple of hours of heavy rain to bring the river up, but this summer was different as it took two days of intermittent north-westerly showers followed by several hours of south-westerly rain before the first spate began. The forestry drainage system, which had been the cause of flash spates for the past twelve years, had obviously become less effective, and it was possible to deduce the cause. In the spring the rows of conifers had been a foot or so apart, but by July the new growth had enabled most of them to close up, turning the forest into a dense skin and preventing the rains from finding a speedy way to the drains. The result was that the spates were quite suddenly reverting to something approaching their former nature, before the coming of the forest. Instead of rising quickly and dropping back within hours, they now began to rise slowly and to run steadily at a more moderate level before slowly dropping back over days. The change was welcome, for it meant longer and more predictable fishing spells as well as partly offsetting the loss of rainwater which is, according to a Welsh study of new forest, approximately forty percent, comprising thirty percent taken by the trees and ten percent by evaporation.

The first spate was a clear one of moderate height. It was late in the afternoon before the water reached a good fishing level, leaving time enough to cover a fair stretch of river either upstream or down. I decided on the latter, and by the time I set off the rain had ceased and the wind died away to a warm

breeze. The river, now running strongly, had already taken on a new and powerful character, covering all but the largest stones in its course, drowning the bright yellow monkey flowers and turning the pool near our door into a heavy run. I saw no trout showing near the surface but guessed there would already be some action going on below.

At the end of the farm there is a big mid-stream boulder which at times shelters a large trout. Its pyramidal tip was now barely showing above the water, and the intervening current was too broad and rapid to fish over. I went on to a small pool at the next bend which holds several good fish. This is one of those difficult ones which only during a spate will give up more than the odd trout; today they were not yet very active, and my worm, though clearly visible across the swollen pool, attracted only a single small fish. Once I had come here with Bill when the water was nicely coloured and the fish at the peak of their spate frenzy. Bill had taken six on the fly, including some good ones in a short spell, to my small one on a worm.

Further down I fished some likely pockets in the open stream, taking another wee one and a nine-incher. The smaller fish had now started feeding, but the larger ones I knew to be there were not yet responding and I went towards the larger pools in the hope that these were in better form. When the bigger fish in the stream become active it is often possible to make a good catch without touching the big pools at all, and I have caught twelve- and thirteen-inchers from little runs barely deep enough to cover their backs.

I crossed the delta of the Polsue burn, running now at two or three times its usual size, and down to the overhang. In high water I usually concentrate on covering a nearside eddy behind the rockface, but I have never had much of a catch there and decided this time to have a look at the pool from the vantage of the overhang. I found that from there I could cover the whole of the small pool without interference from the heavy nearside current, and I tried a cast to the opposite side. The worm landed on gravel in an inch or so of water, but before I could pull it off a small trout had shot up from below, wiggled up the gravel and grabbed it. The fish had come from a deep, steady run on the far side of the main current, a place I had not noticed from water-level, and I wondered whether this was the hotspot I had missed. The next few minutes said that it was, and also showed in classic fashion the behaviour of trout at the peak of spate feeding.

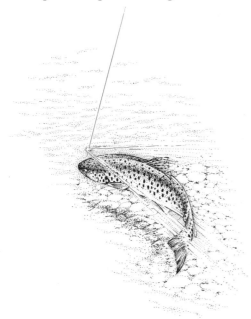

On the next cast the bait landed right at the top of the deeper water, and as it sank there came a good tug. I hauled the fish up hard straight across the surface to the near side and then, trusting my six-pound line, up the rockface – a plump eleven-incher. Next cast the worm drifted only a little farther down before another good one took it hard – a ten-incher

which received the same indelicate removal from the water. The next two casts produced trout of consecutively smaller size and the hotspot now looked fished out, though I felt sure I had missed the pool's big one. Bill once lost a very good fish here which ran down hard towards the tail and snapped the cast. His loss was partly offset in the next pool down, where he caught three trout at once on his team of flies.

After the action at the overhang I now had the better part of a catch. As I went on a mink appeared on the opposite bank, a black one with a white spot on its flank, probably flushed from its lair by the high water. Midges were now rising from the ground, and down by the Midpool they were out in numbers. I stayed long enough to catch five quarter-pounders in quick succession from the slacker water before moving on.

In the next pool there is a spate hotspot, right at the point where the current divides around a rocky island at the tail. Today in the clear water, I did not expect a big catch from it, but as I walked down a couple of heavy rises broke surface. I stopped ten yards up and cast a small worm to the centre of the swollen and gently swirling area, expecting an immediate bite from one of the risers. It came as the bait hit the water, but the fish was another quarter-pounder. When I re-cast, the bait settled on the river-bed for two or three minutes before a touch, and I wondered if the big fish were already turning, as they often do, to take small insects around the surface as the spate subsided. I retrieved fast, and halfway back the bait stopped dead in a heavy swirl. Good fish, I thought, but lightly hooked, since there has been little chance for it to get the bait down before the point was set. I kept the rod steady and the fish, tightening hard against it, swam off fast towards the tail. I hauled hard: it leapt clear of the heavy water at the very lip of the pool, but stayed on and turned off into a slack. It ran off again and jumped twice more, but I kept the pressure on and was soon able to lead it across to a beaching place – a well-formed male of thirteen inches with the hook set lightly in the roof of the mouth.

The midges were now getting troublesome enough to disturb the fishing again. I returned to my spot and immediately missed two bites, both of the fast, strong kind which mean good trout. Cursing the attentions of the insects, I cast again towards the far side of the tail just as a really big fish rose in it. It turned heavily in the water but failed to take the worm twitched in front of it. I brought the line back in long pulls,

84

and as the bait was about to leave the water a large shape came up and snatched it. The rod whipped down but after a few seconds sprang free again. There was a great swirl as the fish, the third big one to take my hook this season, became the second of them to get away.

After this brief encounter the water went quiet. Several times the bait fished through the pool without result, except for a little bat appearing in the dusk and flying into the line. A little later there came another pull, and after letting the fish run off a little I tightened. The line went solid round a boulder so I slacked off to let the trout, if it was still there, swim free. On tightening again there came a thump on the line to say it was still with me and soon another plump eleven-incher lay on the bank.

The river was still running high but, with only the odd fish now rising in the grey dusk, I decided to pack up. My catch, a fairly typical one for four hours' summer spate fishing, consisted of sixteen trout, including three tiny ones, eight fish from four to six ounces, and five from eight to fourteen ounces.

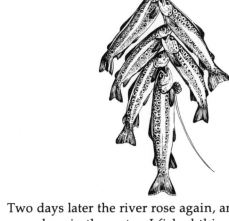

Two days later the river rose again, and this time there was some colour in the water. I fished this spate with Louis, who was able to catch some fish of the size which had eluded him at Goose Island. We had a dozen trout each in a two-hour afternoon spell. Some of the larger fish from these catches had the look of trout from Ken Doon loch. A run of loch fish, mostly ten- to twelve-inchers, ascend the river each summer, and these had the sure distinguishing mark of the Deugh's migratories: several internal cysts, each containing a red, whiplike parasitic worm. This creature, whose hosts at various stages of its lifecycle include snails and birds, rarely affects the condition of the loch fish to any noticeable degree, while those which remain in the river seem to escape infestation entirely.

The loch trout also tend to look slimmer than the river ones, though they do not have the distinctive shape of trout from big still waters. The free-swimming lifestyle of the Loch Doon trout produces a streamlined body with a narrow tailstalk and swallow tail, as well as a pale body colour and sparse spotting. Like sea trout, their tails thicken up when they return to the spawning streams.

I have on previous occasions taken several trout from the overhang pool with an appearance I have not seen elsewhere. I caught them in the deep, fast water against the rockface; they were all light-coloured and covered with small, dense, speckles. The resident Deugh trout with the least number of spots come from slow, deep sections. Below one such stretch I have sometimes caught fish which have moved down into a broad, shallow area to feed or shelter during a spate. The usual trout in this area have the large, numerous spots common to those from the open river, although even these more usual ones have so many variations in spot pattern that no two are quite alike.

The trout with the strongest colours and markings are often those from the small burns. Here a half-pounder will often retain its parr-marks not, as is often supposed, due to poor feeding, but to the part played by these markings in its densely populated environment.

The appearance of spate trout varies in proportion to the amount of colour in the water. They turn progressively paler as the river becomes more opaque, and those from a really dirty spate lose virtually all colour; with faded spots on off-white flanks they lack only the iridescent, silvery glint to bring their appearance to that of a sea trout. After death, their bodies may retain much of their original colour if they are left exposed to the air.

Not all spates fish as well as the ones which ended this year's dry spell. Summer spates may be heavily coloured by tiny fragments of the long algae strands which have built up in low water, or by the erosion of a bankside which turns the water downstream into a brown soup and leaves the sight-hunting trout blind to the angler's offerings. Again, the rain may be heavy enough to turn spate into flood, reducing the angler to dangling a worm in a rare bankside slack. Nevertheless, even these less than ideal spates are preferable to none at all, since often enough they fish well as they are dropping back.

The time of year can also have a considerable effect on the nature of a spate. In early spring, when hill-snows may freeze by night and thaw by day, regular afternoon rises in water level produce the same effect as on glacial streams. North-westerly spates in the early season are too cold to bring the trout strongly on to the feed, and it may be as late as the latter half of June before these fish well. A warm south-westerly, however, is less affected by the season, and it is probable that trout feed well in spates when the wind is in this direction even in winter.

Another typical spate is the one which follows a thunder-storm. This can give a welcome quick rise to the river in settled summer weather although its effects in the watershed can be very uneven. One such August spate came as a complete surprise as there had been no rain at the farm that day and I had seen no sign of the heavy shower which had fallen higher up the valley. Another thunderstorm gave two hours of heavy rain and put the Deugh up to good level in the afternoon. The sudden rise washed out a bank on the upper reaches, turning the river an unusual deep orange; the Bow Burn came up but remained clear, while the Polsue, which the storm evidently missed, remained at its usual level. The river was dropping back again by six o'clock in the evening but remained highly coloured; it was not until eight o'clock that the water started to clear, enabling me to make a catch before darkness. One of the fish, an eight-incher, disgorged two half-grown frogs, and I used the larger as bait to catch a nice half-pounder next cast.

Several other trout I caught that evening contained frogs. Most years there is at least one such frog-spate, usually in July or early August when the river banks are thick with the young of these animals awaiting only a good rise in the river to wash them down to the waiting trout. Spates at other times are often characterized by a predominance of some other creature in the stomachs of the fish: cranefly and caterpillar spates occur every year. Loach spates are a regular occurrence too, and it is

an odd fact that although trout are rarely washed away in high water, the hydrodynamically shaped loach can quite often be found among bankside flotsam as the river subsides.

Although a particular food item may predominate, most spate-caught trout contain a whole range of creatures. Their stomachs will hold one or more types of the usual aquatic nymphs – mayfly, stonefly, or caddis – washed from the river-bed, and often some adult flies as well. Terrestrial insects and their larvae may be even more numerous. Larger creatures commonly include small fish and frogs, but toads, newts, lizards, small birds or mice may turn up in the stomachs of larger fish. There is at least one record of a trout having eaten a fully-grown adder.

The key to what trout will eat, in spates as at other times, appears to be availability. Some fish, however, will concentrate on a particular food item during high-water just as they will during low-water fly hatches. Earthworms seem to be a favourite, and the fullest trout stomachs I have seen contained so many worms that the muscular walls were stretched to transparency. There is a likely reason for this gluttony, since apart from the obviously agreeable taste of earthworms a trout can fill up on their soft bodies without the sharp pressure on their internal organs which the hard parts of almost every other prey item would create.

The feeding behaviour of trout at different stages of a big spate is quite distinctive. Typically, the better fish will start to

Spate-feeding: Typical Riverpool Sequence

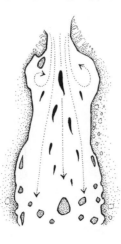

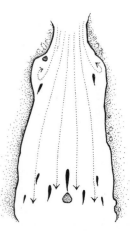

Rising Water
Trout start feeding heavily, with large ones at the head of the pool

Medium Spate
Many fish move down to the tail and continue feeding

congregate at the head of a pool as the water rises, but by the time it is running hard most will move down to the tail. Here they can wait in the less turbulent current for food to be washed down to them, and the concentration of food in the shallow tail may enable the fish to continue feeding even if the water becomes heavily coloured. If spate turns to flood, however, they will move again to find shelter behind large stones or against the banks.

As the water subsides trout move out again from sheltered places to feed in the open water. They often continue feeding hard even if the river drops back to its normal level, some waiting at the neck of the pool while others hunt over the tail for food items deposited there earlier. Occasionally a sheltering fish will be caught out by the falling water and I have several times seen one, awakened by my appearance, swim from an isolated bankside puddle and wriggle at top speed over wet ground down to the river.

While the river is in heavy spate or flood the trout often continue feeding, but locating their shelters can be a problem. One of the best I know on the Deugh is an eddy behind a rock ledge near the head of the farm swimming pool. By moving in against the drystone base of the old footbridge it is possible to fish here with only the rod-tip projecting over the bank: the first time I tried it in high water I took a dozen trout in an hour, including a half-pounder containing a fully grown vole. This convenient spot proved another ideal one for beginners,

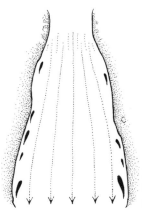

Full Spate or Flood
*Current forces trout
to shelter*

Falling Water
*Fish move about,
picking up food
deposited by spate or
awaiting current-
bourne items*

and in the following seasons several people caught their first trout here, all during high water, except for two boys who found they could take a fish or two when the river was at a low level by fishing into the darkness.

A particular advantage of this place is that it can be fished successfully without the usual accoutrements of the modern angler – in particular the fixed-spool reel which is little better than an impediment to beginners and young children. Here they can use a simple pole and fixed line to good effect. The little hazel on the Bow Burn produces a nice rod every year or so, and it is on one of these that many catches have been made. There are some larger waters where this old-fashioned pole method can also be used successfully. A friend of mine used a long willow pole on his first visit to a big river; fishing in heavy, coloured water he caught two brown trout, one weighing eight ounces, the other eight pounds.

Short, sharp spates can be good for the fisher who lives by the water, but it takes a big south-westerly to bring anglers out in numbers from the towns. For many the wild, wet days which dismay the summer visitor are all too few, and it is hardly an exaggeration to say that the worse the weather the more anglers will be out in it.

In an area which has enough variety in wild trout fishing to suit any angler's taste, the quality of that on the remoter reaches of the Deugh is not sufficient to attract many visitors, and we are lucky to see one a year at the farm. When he does appear, it is usually during typical south-westerly weather with misty, ragged clouds racing low over the hills and the rain coming hard with every gust. The infrequent appearance of such a man does not mean that he is a casual visitor. It is likely that he will have once lived in the area, the economic conditions which caused his family to move away to Dalmellington or New Cumnock not preventing him from continuing to fish the waters of his youth.

His technique, taught him by his father, is the traditional wet-fly. If the water is already high he will fish downstream, slowly and methodically, his short line covering every run and pocket. His movements show economy, and his powerful rod – doubling, perhaps, for both trout and salmon – lifts the line from the water and puts it down again in a single easy movement. When a trout comes at his fly he shows no sign of it, leaving the fish to tighten against the rod and then hustling it from the water with a minimum of effort. His simply tied flies are variations of long-proven patterns: a black one with a red tail and two speckled brownish kinds – one with a twist of gold tinsel along it and the other with a body of peacock herl – would be typical. Neither his tackle nor technique owes much of importance to the angling innovations of the past century, but it is unlikely for his catch to have felt the lack of them; since his choice of fishing conditions is usually correct by the time he reaches the farm he will already have taken a selection of good Deugh trout.

Downstream wet-fly fishing, though still practised on many moorland streams, continues to come in for criticism by devotees of newer and more fashionable methods. Two contradictory arguments are used against it, one stating that it takes too few trout, the other that it takes too many. The first is put forward by those people who have probably never seen it used in the traditional manner but who presume it is easier to approach the fish and hook them by working upstream. In clear-water conditions this is obviously so, but the traditional downstream fisher, who knows well enough which way the trout face, rarely bothers with clear-water angling. He goes out when the water is high, when the trout are feeding hard and he can cover them with deadly effect at close range.

The second argument, that this method takes too many trout, is presumably put forward by those who do know of its effectiveness under the correct conditions. The restrictions in angling methods on some overfished waters, or those with no spawning facilities, are not nearly so useful where typical spate streams are concerned. Many hill streams need a good fishing pressure to keep the numbers of trout down and the average size up, and these are better off without any restrictions on technique.

It may seem strange that traditional fly-fishing methods are relatively little publicized as not only are they still widely practised but they have been the basis for many new methods used on different waters. Although flies may now be dressed in all sorts of ways, the names and colours of many patterns used throughout the world attest to their origins on the moorland waters of Britain. It may be that many anglers today prefer whatever is new for its own sake and look upon older methods, however effective, as something archaic and backward, without realizing that the basics of angling have changed very little over the centuries.

Perhaps the very effectiveness of the old-fashioned spate-

stream and loch methods, both fly and bait, work against current trends of fishing. Pompous arguments are sometimes advanced for the separation of anglers into sport and meat fishermen, a divisive idea which works against the appreciation of angling as a whole. Fortunately Scotland is still relatively free of such nonsense, fishers here having no problem in getting the most out of their sport while also taking pleasure in returning home with a good catch. Those few who pride themselves in returning their fish alive are regarded as little short of fools. Not only do such people lay themselves open to the arguments of anti-angling groups thereby threatening their own sport, but they also deny themselves the satisfaction of providing fresh food of a quality rarely available in the shops.

In my own case any separation between sport and food-fishing would be particularly inappropriate, since for many seasons trout have provided the major source of protein for my family. It is hardly a coincidence that my average fishing spell of ninety minutes is also the average time it takes me to amass a meal. If I had not taken trout for food I would hardly have been able to justify my angling at all, and apart from the possibility of losing a wife I would not have been able to make the studies which are necessary to my work. While the importance of using fishing time productively in terms of food may have encouraged my addiction to worm fishing, I doubt if this has interfered with the overall pleasure I obtain from a fascinating sport.

One result of eating a lot of trout is that this fish is regarded in my house as a staple food rather than a luxury. Variety in cooking methods has become important so we prepare trout in several ways. Frying is reserved for the red-fleshed ones over twelve inches, except in July when the smaller ones are at the peak of fatness prior to development of spawn and roe. Those are fried plain or in the traditional way, rolled in oatmeal, ideally after being left overnight with salt in the body cavity. Small ones at other times of the year are usually made into tasty troutcakes, and over the season we often eat more prepared this way than any other.

In July and August this year I had some good catches out of which most of the larger trout were saved for a fish-fry with our neighbours. We had amassed a heap of ten to twelve-inchers, two red-fleshed pounders and a big one, plus a couple of large perch – part of a twenty-five-fish catch Jim and I had made one wet day on Loch Doon. These were grilled and part-smoked over an outdoor fire of Bow Burn rowan wood on a similar showery afternoon and eaten indoors by seven children and fourteen adults, including the whole population of the upper valley and several summer visitors.

CHAPTER SEVEN

Kings and Queens

A pound trout is a good one on most hill waters, and the
Deugh is no exception. Bill and I have been content with one
or two such fish annually from around the farm, each coming
as a bonus, perhaps, to a good spate or evening catch. During
the first few seasons on the Deugh we never saw one much
over this size; although there were stories of much bigger
trout having been taken, we assumed that they had been rare
freaks from Ken Doon loch.

It was Bill who first made contact with the mysterious big
trout. One afternoon he saw two lying in the shallow, sunlit
tail of the swimming pool, the smaller of which he reckoned at
twice the size of the usual middle Deugh maximum. The
following summer he hooked a big one on a fly which
although it broke free was another indication that such fish
may actually be commoner than we had supposed.

It was on a later September evening that Bill hooked a
second large fish. He had cast a silver spinner to the neck of
the Midpool in the last of the light and, as it spashed down,
the fish snatched it from the surface of the fast water and ran
off downstream. This time it stayed on and was successfully
landed – a sixteen-inch female: small-headed and finely
formed, this queen of the pool was the first proof that the
middle river could produce a trout approaching two pounds in
weight. Several miles downstream, beyond the Green Well of
Scotland, such fish are taken more regularly. There is a good
stretch of day-ticket water on the lower Deugh, but in spite of
its proximity to a road the fishing pressure remains moderate,
and this part of the river probably has the best average size of
fish on the whole water.

For some years Bill and I were too occupied with the fishing
around the farm to bother with other stretches. When we did
visit a new one it was not downstream but to the upper
reaches we went, above the small dam which siphons off
water to the Galloway hydro network. The dam is a fairly
unobtrusive sign of man's interest in the river apart from its

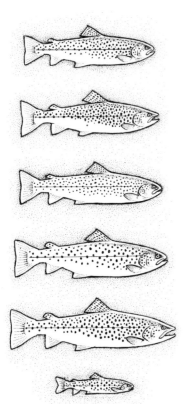

Scale Drawings of five big Deugh trout showing shape and condition.
From the top:
16-inch, 1½ lbs September
16½-inch, 1¾ lbs July
17-inch, 2 lbs June
18½-inch, 2¾ lbs June
20-inch, 3lbs June
Bottom: Average 9-inch trout

fish, but nonetheless it has a significant influence on the trout. Like countless small dams elsewhere it has no fish-pass, a testament to the ignorance of law-makers regarding the supposedly non-migratory nature of the brown trout. On many rivers the largest fish spawn in the highest reaches, and there can be little doubt that were such obstructions on trout streams made passable the fish traffic between head waters and the lochs, rivers and sea below would add to the quality of the fishing.

This particular dam has another more serious effect as a consequence of its abstraction system. In showery weather this carries away the extra water from the upper river and it takes heavy rain before a rise in the level tops the overflow and brings its benefits to the reaches below. Over the past few seasons trout in the first miles above the dam have averaged half the weight again of those in the middle reaches, a difference which may be largely due to the fewer spates below.

The first time Bill and I fished the upper river was during a south-westerly spate one July. It was still raining when we arrived, several miles upstream, to find it already turning to flood and giving these steeper reaches the appearance of a Himalayan torrent. We fished our flies for a while, but the water continued to rise and there soon seemed but one hope for a fish. I turned over some stones, found a large pink worm and, having draped it over my fly, dropped it into the only available spot – a tiny run a foot or so deep under a nearby bank. I hooked into a good trout immediately, a nice thirteen-incher, which encouraged further visits in better conditions.

Since then we have gone upriver once or twice each season, and although it was some time before we saw a trout there larger than that first one, we heard reports of a couple of over two pounds being taken. In one pool big fish had twice been hooked and lost, once by the father-in-law of Davy McKay, the shepherd, and another time by the forest keeper, whose fly was taken at the head of the pool in a summer spate by a trout which had the unmistakeable feel of a large one.

Last year Bill and I went up on the spur of the moment to try this spot during a rising spate in early June. The rain had abated to a fine drizzle, but this rather undistinguished-looking pool was running high with foam-flecks showing white against the dark, peaty water. We had a choice of tackle with us but the river looked right for any method; Bill put up his fly-rod and went down towards the tail, where a few fish were beginning to rise to adult stoneflies, while I went up to the neck to fish a worm.

Our first casts brought no response. I was fishing from a small promontory up into the heavy water, and after a few minutes I moved a couple of yards down to try a new angle. As I prepared to cast there was a splash from upstream, and a few feet from where I had just been standing there was a slashing

rise and I caught a glimpse of a broad back. It was the classic rise of a big fish, and I realized that this could be the only opportunity of the season to hook one.

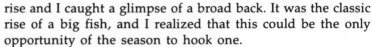

I put a second worm on and cast cautiously over the spot. The current whipped it back downstream so I cast again a few feet further up, keeping loose line in my left hand while remaining in touch with the bait as it came down in mid-water. Again there was no offer, nor on the next cast, which made me wonder if the fish had already become suspicious. On the fourth cast I sent the bait several yards further still, giving it time to sink deep, and as it reached the promontory area the line stopped dead. When I tightened, a fish came across the current with an odd sliding motion and, with barely any resistance, arrived deep in the water under the rod. It felt like a small one, but when I started to haul upwards there came two heavy tugs as the trout, suddenly awakening to the pressure of its jaw, tried to shake the hook free. Failing this, it swam steadily off across the current in a way which left no doubt about its size. The rod bent hard over and stayed there as the reel sang its song. Bill went downstream to get his net; when the fish also surged downstream I overtook him at a run, stopping halfway down the pool as the trout halted to fight it out. It made several fast, head-shaking runs around the middle of the pool and then suddenly leapt out, looking improbably large and bright against the black water: some-how it felt as though the fish's power was an embodiment of the pool itself. It leapt a second time, seeming to hang in the air poised for inspection.

After a while the big trout began holding a few yards out, and Bill put the net down. He had replaced a damaged net bag with a new one the previous night, and I was glad he had done so, for the river had drowned the gravel bars which would otherwise have allowed me to beach the fish. Under pressure it came up beneath the rod and rolled on its side, but this was no ordinary trout, for it righted itself again and swam off downstream with all the power of its first run. I chased it as it headed for the broken water beyond the tail, down towards the spot where, many years ago, a summer spate had washed away a coffin being taken across the river by horse and cart. Before it got to the tail I stopped and put on full pressure; for a moment everything went solid, then the fish came around slowly, across the current and into the margin. It refused to show its flanks again but it was beaten now, and Bill made no mistakes with the net as he lifted it out of the water and onto the bank.

We stopped on the roadside and examined the catch. It looked very deep, and its perfect shape and immaculate fins reflected its condition. It had the silvery look of a typical spate fish, although the usual patch of emerald behind the eye continued as a pale iridescent streak along the lateral line, and there was a lilac tint to its upper flanks. I looked at the head expecting to recognize the creature's sex, and was surprised by its appearance. The sex of most Deugh trout can be recognized by the time they reach maturity at nine or ten inches, but this one had the small head and rounded snout of a hen while its shoulders had the hump of a cock fish. On the strength of its expression, which was rather bullish, I guessed it to be a male, which it turned out to be.

As we sat admiring the trout a figure moving with the fast, purposeful stride of a shepherd appeared upstream, and we were joined by Davy, halfway round his ten-mile daily circuit. 'Well,' he said, looking at the fish, 'that's the biggest trout I've seen out of the Deugh yet – and look, there's its mate.' We turned to see the rings of a heavy rise near the tail of the pool, whose productivity seemed all the more impressive when he told us of another big one, a two-pounder, taken here on the first day of the season.

Davy is no sport-fisher, although like most hill shepherds he can catch himself a meal in a spate. He has an eye, too, for the changes which have been taking place in the Deugh trout-fishing over the years. Before the arrival of the mink the fish were more numerous than today, and he remembers a time when New Cumnock anglers would walk over the hills in the evening, take good night catches down the length of the upper river, and walk over the hill into the next valley to catch the morning bus home. This trip, comprising a ten-mile walk and a bus ride of similar length, has now been largely replaced by shorter visits in motor cars by members of the New Cumnock angling association, the club which has long had the fishing on the upper river.

He has seen other changes too, including the transformation of much of the hill country from open moorland to forest. Davy still lives only three miles from Waterhead, the ancestral home of the clan MacAdam where he and Davy Murdoch, the last shepherds to live in the upper valley, stayed in the last years of its shepherding community.

Signs of human activity in the days long before the sheep farms can be seen in the valley's ancient remains. Long ago, the MacAdams doubtless followed the way of life common to other parts of Scotland and which can still be seen in mountains and deserts of other countries. The pastoral existence and semi-isolation of the people would have been rewarded through long ages, not just by beautiful surroundings, but by their relative freedom from the burdens of more feudal agricultural and urban societies of the lowlands. The coming of the big sheep farms would have hastened changes in the age-old power structure of the clan, as they did in the Highlands, with allegiance to chieftains giving way to mere economic dependence on landlords. Many inhabitants would have been forced from their holdings to make way for the sheep, especially when the enclosures of estates highlighted their locations.

When Davy first came here the glen had a traditional character in spite of the changes. The geography and common occupation of the people of the valley may have helped to retain its pastoral atmosphere. Changes, however, relentlessly continued as people left to make their fortunes in the towns or distant countries and were replaced by a succession of temporary shepherds. Meanwhile, the area had attracted the interests of big-business concerns. Galloway's huge hydro-electric system reached the area, the Deugh dam was built, and along with it came the upper valley's short stretch of surfaced road. After the war, a public afforestation scheme was started, and later concessions for private forestry companies led to a new and impersonal interest in the hills. Land prices soared, farming interests lost out and by the mid-1970s the map of Galloway had become a huge patchwork of hastily planned forests interspersed with remaining patches of sheepwalk. This development was the last straw for small upland communities, and tenant shepherds lost work and home in one move. In the Deugh valley, just when the road could have brought new life here, the dozen or so shepherding families were replaced by a forest manager and a gamekeeper; when extra labour was needed it was obtained on a casual basis from outside.

For the hill people of Scotland the economic progress of the past three hundred years seems to have worked in reverse. With every step has come a decline in population and increased economic dependence on outside interests, so that in spite of the progress made in agricultural methods the uplands

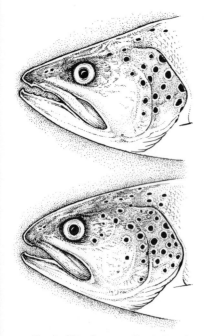

Typical head proportions of cock and hen trout:
16½-inch male (above)
17-inch female (below)

support only a fraction of their population of a thousand years ago. Industrial society, which at first benefited from the changes, seems meanwhile to have found itself out on an increasingly perilous limb, although even now it tends to see the countryside only in terms of holiday visits. One way ahead would be a programme to encourage smallholdings, not only in the new forests and government-owned land, but on the big upland estates as well. The aim would not be to involve newcomers in some semi-feudal tie to a landlord, but to give them the opportunity of the kind of independent rights which could work towards true revilatization of country life.

Perhaps the trout, after all, are quite well off in spite of the new hazards of mink, dams and drainage ditches. At least they still manage to live here, and the clan-line of my big one doubtless goes back unbroken to the first trout entering the Dee estuary in the wake of the retreating ice sheets, and their attendant packs of arctic char, several thousand years ago. Though isolated, this fish's forefathers would never have been in need of new stock. They would also have remained unaffected by 'outside interests' whether feudal or democratic, communist or capitalist; in particular, not one chubby, lop-tailed representative of the totalitarian regime of the fish-farm would ever have reached here.

Since our introduction to the big fish of the Deugh it has become increasingly obvious that although many remain uncaught, each of the big settling pools holds at least one of them. They reach their unusual size by becoming absolute masters of their space, taking the prime feeding stations in big insect hatches or during spates and hunting lesser fishes when the current fails to provide. These prey fishes may be of prime importance to their exceptionally fast growth, the favourite among Deugh trout being the stone loach. This prolific fish has a high oil content, and since it commonly grows to four or five inches it represents a good meal for a two-pounder. A characteristic of the big trout is the speed with which they overtake their brethren in size, and I have seen only one in the middle-class category between one pound two ounces and one pound eight ounces. Eight big ones caught in recent years were taken by all three common angling methods, bait, fly and spinner, and averaged a little over two and a quarter pounds each.

How big the Deugh trout could grow can, as on other waters, only be guessed at. Certainly four- and five-pounders

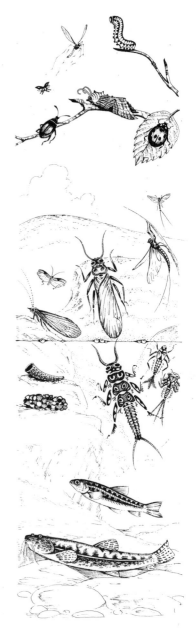

Typical diet of Deugh trout
Bottom: Loach and minnow
Centre: Main types of aquatic insect, larvae and winged adults. From the left caddis, stonefly, mayfly.
Top: Seasonal terrestrial insects

have been taken, as glass-cased specimens in New Cumnock testify. They were mostly caught before the dam was built, in a big pool now just downstream; and the upper river produced a six-pounder to a worm for the grandfather of one angler from that town.

The largest brown trout recorded in recent years in the local Glenkens area was a nine-pounder, caught on a puddock, or frog, from a Loch Ken tributary burn in late September. Not far away are the sea trout rivers, some of which produce silver monsters of twenty pounds, while further north the big Highland lochs hold even larger fish, the char-fed ferox which has long made British angling records and may grow to forty pounds or more.

Some of the biggest trout in Europe come from similar char or whitefish lakes in Finland or in the Alps, where one over twenty-seven kilograms was taken in commercial nets. This one was still far from being a record *salmo trutta*, however, since the Caspian race has produced many in excess of a hundred pounds. L. S. Berg, the Russian taxonomist, recorded one of a hundred and twelve pounds on a visit to the Caspian Sea, a weight exceeding that recorded for any other salmonid fish except the Chinook salmon, which has been recorded to at least a hundred and twenty-six pounds, and the largest living species – the Siberian taimen – which had been known to reach a hundred and sixty-five pounds. Among extinct species, fossils from Oregon have shown that a plankton-feeding salmon once existed in the Pacific which reached estimated weights of over two hundred pounds.

The enormous size which brown trout may reach highlights one of the aspects which make the fish such a fascinating source of study. Berg reckoned the 'Caspian salmon' to be a separate species possessing characteristics of both trout and Atlantic salmon, and it is only in recent years that chromosome studies have shown it to be a trout. Many another taxonomist has had problems in trying to classify local varieties of trout, some having staked their reputations on arguments for or against regarding it as a single species. It is hardly surprising that many have regarded the salmon-like sea trout, with its smolting young, as being inherently different from the tiny, colourful residents of the burns. There is obviously some genetic difference between them, but such differences have never been sufficient to prove satisfactorily the existence of more than one species.

The influence of environment has often been misunderstood by laboratory-oriented students of the trout. One result has been that practical anglers have often had a clearer idea than scientists of environmental effects, since those who fish many waters can hardly fail to notice that similar waters, however far apart, produce similar-looking trout. At one time I

used to fish a head-water burn of Afghanistan's Surkhab River, a tributary of the Oxus at the south-eastern extreme of the brown trout's native range. The colourful appearance of these Central Asian trout was indistinguishable from those of the Bow Burn, several thousand miles away at the north-western end of its range, and I needed no textbook to prove that I was dealing with the same fish.

A major key to the trout's character lies in its colours and markings, but many researchers have decided that these, being variable, are 'unscientific'. In fact, field studies in trout colouration, such as anglers may unconsciously carry out, again provide a clue to the importance of environmental influences, for they make much more sense than purely anatomical studies of dead fish would indicate. It is not so long since some scientists regarded the trout itself as being colour-blind, an idea which made a mockery of centuries of experimentation with artificial flies, and it is indicative of the gap which has grown up between anglers and fishery researchers that such a theory could ever have become popular.

After a century of controversy taxonomists are finally coming to an agreement over the status of the brown trout. Chromosome counts have shown that throughout its range it has the same basic genetic make-up, while at the same time different waters have their own varieties which, while they do have some distinct genetic differences, are largely the product of environment. This one-in-many character of the trout has long been appreciated in Turkey, where both brown and sea trout are called *Allah-bolac*, the Godfish, a creature which symbolizes the Attributes of the One God. In the city of Urfa, birthplace of the Prophet Abraham, trout are kept in ornamental pools together with another fish of symbolic importance, the carp. Africa's only native salmonid, the brown trout of the Atlas torrents, is also honoured by protection in the neighbourhood of a mountain shrine. The symbolic qualities of the trout, however, are not the only ones to be appreciated in Asia and Africa, as there it is also a popular eating fish, particularly the sea trout of the Black, Caspian and Aral seas.

Native range of brown trout

There is a saying among the Japanese, for whom fish have an important cultural as well as economic significance, that the greatest honour a fish can have is to be caught and eaten by man. If this is so, my big one from the upper Deugh should have been duly honoured, not only by being caught and eaten, but by the treatment it received after it had been killed, which was no less formal than that given to a sea trout or salmon.

After catching it, we stopped at Jim's for tea and there the trout was laid out and photographed. Continuing the journey, we showed it to Alan, Davy's neighbour, whom we met on the track to the farm. On arrival home, it was weighed and measured: eighteen and a half inches long and just over two and three-quarter pounds. It was then laid out on our table for the rest of the afternoon.

Before supper the fish received its final preparation. Laying it on a piece of cardboard I made an outline drawing and, cutting off the fins, laid them down in the appropriate places on the outline. The next step was to cut it open, exposing the bright orange flesh. Under its backbone was a roe-sac, which, though undeveloped at that time of year, was enough to identify it positively as a male. Then I cut open its stomach, bulging with spate food, and found the contents so recognizable that there was no need to float them out in a saucer of water for identification. It contained six loach and a mass of adult stoneflies. Removing the insides, I scraped the dark red kidney out from along the backbone, and removed the head for future use as a drawing reference. Lastly I divided the body into two fillets by cutting from the centre of the back down over the ribs on each side. When fried they were so oily that the addition of a little butter was a formality only; the big trout's delicate flavour was as much appreciated as the stron-

ger one of a nice grilse which came for dinner a few weeks later.

A notable feature of all the big trout has been their excellent condition and lack of ugly features often associated with such 'cannibals'. The eighteen-incher was the largest of four big Deugh trout I have caught in the past five seasons. Over the same period Bill, who had fished less often than I, hooked two, but both had escaped by leaping from the water, shaking their heads and throwing the hook. This year, however, he had a distinct change of fortune.

On a windy evening in early June he stopped by a big pool to throw a Mepps spinner across the neck. Second cast it stopped dead and his little telescopic rod whipped over as a big trout bored into the depths. It stayed deep, shaking its head and making several runs, but this time the fish was well hooked and he was presently able to bring to net a fine male trout twenty inches long and over three pounds in weight. Exceptional though it was, this hill-stream monster was not the only big trout Bill had this year. Later in the season, while fishing the outlet of a remote hill loch, he was to hook a much larger one. It fought long and hard, and when it was finally exhausted I had the honour of landing for him a brown trout over two feet long; enormously deep in the body, spotted like a leopard and with a great hooked jaw, this fish had the classic features of a Scottish ferox.

CHAPTER EIGHT

Autumn Moods

The rain showers which ended the long dry spell went on to bring a fairly typical wet end to the summer. Nevertheless, it remained warm and there were few signs of the seasonal change to come, except in the maturing of natural vegetation. On the hill slopes bracken patches began to show orange among the pastel shades of ripening grasses, while wild flowers, particularly the heather, reflected a final glory. July had seen the blooming of the brilliant bell heather, and in August, hillsides and forest breaks were bright with larger areas of the soft mauve ling variety.

Late summer is a quiet time in the valley. Curlew and oystercatcher have now fallen silent; they are among the first birds to arrive and the first to leave, and in August there are no regular bird calls to replace their loud cries. Even on still days the sound of birds is now barely noticeable, being limited, perhaps, to the distant croak of a raven, the brief clucking of a red grouse coming in to land, or towards the end of the month, the cries of small birds gathering for journeys to faraway places.

As migratory birds prepare to leave the Galloway hills the migratory fishes are arriving, and for the next few weeks each spate will bring trout and salmon up from sea, loch and river. The Deugh, though denied the blessing of sea-run fish, reflects the largesse of the season, and the advent of September marks the start of the most fruitful month of the year. It is not only in the presence of loch-run trout that September excels, but also in the increased average size of the resident fish. The seven-inch trout so common in early season have now doubled in weight, so that in spite of the appearance in catches of some little yearlings the predominance of eight- and nine-inchers, plus the arrival of bigger fish from downstream, now make for heavier bags.

In September the trout begin to rise more freely in the day-time than they do in August, but their altered behaviour may be less related to any increase in fly hatches than to

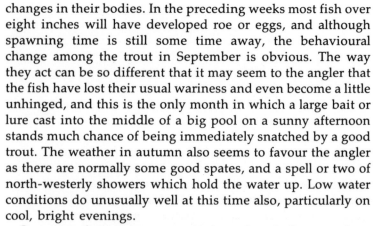

changes in their bodies. In the preceding weeks most fish over eight inches will have developed roe or eggs, and although spawning time is still some time away, the behavioural change among the trout in September is obvious. The way they act can be so different that it may seem to the angler that the fish have lost their usual wariness and even become a little unhinged, and this is the only month in which a large bait or lure cast into the middle of a big pool on a sunny afternoon stands much chance of being immediately snatched by a good trout. The weather in autumn also seems to favour the angler as there are normally some good spates, and a spell or two of north-westerly showers which hold the water up. Low water conditions do unusually well at this time also, particularly on cool, bright evenings.

One year there came a succession of such fine evenings through the final month of the angling season. I fished the sunset hour on ten of them, and catches over the period were unusually consistent. I never came away without at least one trout over the half-pound, and my total of forty fish weighed together over twenty-pounds, all taken from the same spot at the tail of a big pool.

The first visit was on 31 August, the last day of a dry spell which had allowed strings of algae up to twenty feet long to develop in the shallow stretches of the river. I arrived at about five in the afternoon with Nicholas, a neighbour's son who was learning to fish; as we settled down, a bright sun warming the late afternoon air, I put a small worm on the hook, fixed a lead shot a yard above it, cast down to the tail of the pool and, leaving the line slack, set the rod down on a flat ledge beside us. It was rather early yet for the better trout to be moving into the area and although there were no fish rising there a bite came straightaway. It produced a nine-incher, and Nicholas immediately caught another of similar size. We took it in turns to strike the fish, action coming with almost every cast. By dusk we had killed fourteen trout averaging nearly half-a-pound (the largest a three-quarter-pounder) all of them from a few square yards along the tail of the pool, except for a single half-pounder which rose in the slack water to the left and fell for the worm which was immediately cast over it.

Throughout September the pattern of fishing continued. Twice a week I would fish the sunset hour, arriving at the pool just as the sun left the water to cast a worm into the tail. I placed it in front of a stone which has a depression beside it

made by the trout which move in at this time to await food
brought down by the drift. In the clear, shallow water the bait
was rarely taken at once and I found it best to leave it to settle
for a minute or so; if by then a trout had failed to respond I
gave it a very small pull, and as often as not this was when the
first fish went for it. Mostly it was an eight- or nine-incher,
but the next one, as the shadows climbed up the bank, would
usually be larger. Sometimes there would be a quiet spell
when the trout, though rising in the tail, refused to take, and I
would let the bait lie awhile.

In the dusk hour there is often quite a lot going on around
this pool. A mink may appear, cutting a V across the surface,
briefly disturbing the trout as it passes through the tail; or a
blackface ewe grazing on the bank above will start up suddenly and go running off up the hill. A few feet to the left of my
usual fishing position is a marginal sandbar favoured by a
shoal of minnows; after sunset there is sometimes a sudden
splash and swirl as a large trout hits the sandbar, half strands
itself for a moment, and turns away with a small fish clamped
in its jaws. At dusk a pair of carrion crows appear, flying
slowly upstream towards a big rowan where they spend the
night. A family of mallards or mergansers often land on the
pool, and as it gets dark a kestrel flies to its roost in an old
hawthorn on the bank above. That autumn I had usually made
my catch by the time the kestrel arrived.

An interesting feature of the September catches that year
was the proportion of males and females. Of the fish over ten
inches, eleven of the last twelve I took were males, and it may
be that the tails of pools fish well in September due partly to
the aggressive behaviour of the trout before spawning. Mature
males develop thickened anal and lower tail fins at this time,
further signs, perhaps, of their early presence over the shallow
gravels in the pool tails.

It is in the deepest parts of the pools that trout sometimes
display their distracted autumn behaviour most obviously.
Several times I have fished in the late afternoon, casting into
deep water and taking fish after fish on both natural and
artificial lures at all points between the surface and the
river-bed.

Spinning is particularly successful on the Deugh in September, using bigger patterns than the tiny ones which can be so
deadly during summer fly-hatches. Trout seem to eat other
fish more regularly now than in any other month, and I have

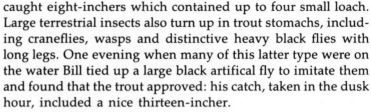

caught eight-inchers which contained up to four small loach. Large terrestrial insects also turn up in trout stomachs, including craneflies, wasps and distinctive heavy black flies with long legs. One evening when many of this latter type were on the water Bill tied up a large black artifical fly to imitate them and found that the trout approved: his catch, taken in the dusk hour, included a nice thirteen-incher.

Towards the end of the season I spend an evening or two over my diaries, comparing the Deugh fishing to that of previous years. Since the details of my fishing – times, places and methods – are pretty consistent, the most interesting facts to emerge are mostly those relating to changes in the sizes and numbers of trout. I keep a note of the size of every one caught and comparisons of these over a season, and then between seasons, provide interesting material for study as well as inspiration for an occasional theory to account for changes in trout population.

One four-year period was particularly interesting. The first year the average size of fish was 9½ inches, about normal, but in the second year it went down to 8½ inches and, in the third year, to 7½ inches. In the fourth year the average went up again to nine inches. An interesting fact about the two poor years was that although small fish predominated in both of them, the second year also showed a distinct lack of medium-sized eight- to ten-inchers, while in the third year there was a lack of ten- to twelve-inchers. It appeared that a whole year-class of fish had somehow been decimated. Scale reading confirmed that for the most part the eight- to ten-inch category consisted of two-year-olds, and the ten- to twelve-inch of three-year-olds; the missing medium-sized trout in the second year, the two-year-olds, had become the missing large fish of the third year.

The reason for this loss of fish was a mystery. As far as we knew the river had never been polluted, and even if it had, it seemed unlikely that only fish of a certain age group would be affected. Nor had there been any unusual influx of predators, such as mergansers or mink, which could account for a loss of small fish. There had, however, been two very big November floods just after the eggs of this year-class would have been laid, and these seemed the likeliest cause of its disappearance. One flood was memorable; it was the largest in at least ten years, and washed away the protective embankment which Bill had made at the bottom of his garden. It also took away an

old washing machine which ended up way downstream in a favourite pool of his where it continued to serve him in the unlikely capacity of an anti-poaching device, I myself having lost a good trout under it.

Another thing which scale-reading confirmed was the fast growth rate of the big Deugh trout. Instead of stopping at thirteen or fourteen inches like most trout, these shot ahead, reaching around two pounds while relatively young. The two-and -three-quarter-pounder was only a few weeks past its fifth birthday, and its growth rate was practically identical with that given by Frost and Brown for the fast-growing trout of the river Test.

I also keep an annual list of notable trout, which on the Deugh means fish of ten inches and over. I include details of sex, stomach content and any other interesting facts; although this list is of less overall interest than the more general one it is more fun to fill in after returning from fishing. An interesting side to this list is the location of captures. Two favourite pools produce thirty or forty half-pound-plus trout between them year after year, and the records suggest that heavy fishing has made no difference to the pools' productivity. The regular movements of trout on the river doubtless lead to a pretty immediate re-stocking of such pools, but their ability to grow trout in the quantities they do is in stark contrast to the low yields of the land round about. Textbooks equate the productivity of the so-called poor acid streams which lie at the heart of Britain's huge moorland trout fishery to that of the best arable land, and the productivity of river settling pools is probably higher again. On the burns, it takes only an hour or two to make an effective 'half-pounder pool' with boulders, and it is interesting to speculate on the boom in wild trout production which a few thousand such dams could create. This may occur only if trout were to become an important food. Should the oceans continue to be polluted at the current rate the hill-streams, which now suffer an unprecedented neglect, may yet prove important in new methods of trout production. Meanwhile the wild hill-waters remain the domain of the fortunate few who find here, at practically no material disadantage to themselves, fishing of a kind infinitely more exciting than that of stocked trout fisheries of the lowlands.

Alec is one person who makes regular trips after the wild trout of the hills. Since our April meeting by the lochs I had not seen him, but we met in September and exchanged some tales of the season. He had continued his stocking of selected lochans, and his work had been rewarded by the capture on a fly of a fine hen trout of three and a half pounds. Another catch had come from a remote burn which runs for several miles between lochs in another part of the Rhinns. Not long after our last meeting he had stopped there to fish a familiar pool, and as he did so he noticed that its usual light-coloured, sandy bed had turned dark. He soon disccovered that he was seeing not the bottom of the pool but the solid-packed backs of an extraordinary spring migration of wild trout; he took a record catch of forty-nine fish, all over the half-pound, from that one spot. He returned next day with his brother and in a short session before the weather closed in they took a further eighteen trout on fly and spinner, the largest of them weighing a pound and two ounces.

As September advanced the abundance of autumn was making itself felt everywhere. The red berries of the rowans were reaching a peak of brilliance, while blackberries and rosehips, some of them destined for winter preserves, adorned the hedgerows of the lower valleys. The gardens were now producing some of the best vegetables of the year, while larger farming operations were busy with late crop-harvesting and preparations for sale of the year's grown lambs.

The signs of autumn were obvious indoors too. Our window-sill aquarium was thick with the season's growth of waterplants, while the occupants of the numerous spiders' webs on our walls were starting their autumn courting activities. Over the season they had grown from tiny and barely noticeable creatures into quite substantial residents, their backs marked with the conspicuous dotted cross of the garden spider. For months they had remained at their webs, doing a useful job on the flies and midges, but now they were taking more interest in each other. The slender males began to work their way clockwise round the upper walls and ceiling, stopping hesitantly to twang the webs of the impressively plump females and attempting to approach them closer by means of leg-signals. This was evidently a sensitive manoeuvre, for usually the male would suddenly turn and flee, leaving the game to the one following behind while he went on to check out the next web. There was obviously danger involved too, for many males had one or more hind legs missing.

The aquarium had been set up in the summer as a sort of

miniature lochan. Sarah had contributed a collection of multi-coloured stones to line the bottom and I got some plants for it from the garden pools – water forget-me-not, pondweed, water plantain and water crowfoot. We then went down to the river with a tea-sieve and collected some wildlife, including scaly mayfly nymphs, caddis larvae, tadpoles, and fourteen minnows including ten tiny half-inch fry, three medium-sized ones and a three-inch-plus monster. We filled the little plastic tank with water from the garden burn, and the plants and animals settled down in it immediately.

After a day or two some mayflies, spurred on perhaps by the new warmth, started to emerge, and they continued on for weeks. An empty nymph shell would appear at the edge of a leaf, and on the window above there would be a plump new dun complete with wings and tail-whisks. Within a day or so the dun would split its skin and out would come the fly in its final state: the delicate spinner, shimmering with iridescent colour. Meanwhile the caddis, which had been munching their way around the plants like a flock of sheep, also began to hatch, and in the evenings one or two of them, joined perhaps by others from outside, would flutter round our lamp.

The tadpoles sprouted legs, lost tails and emerged from the tank as small frogs. The minnow fry turned into a shoal of plump and glittering little fish, with regular patrol routes through the plant forest; after dinner they would wait in a clear patch for a pinch of breadcrumbs to arrive. The water-plants hardly seemed to notice the change of environment, and their fast growth doubtless helped to keep the water well oxygenated for the animals. By September the stony bed had become coated with a thick layer of algae, its filaments now spreading up among the rooted plants to give the tank the appearance of what some call eutrophication.

Louis had also been keeping an aquarium, an even smaller one in the form of a large jar. The star of his show was a gigantic *Dytiscus* water beetle, its glittering gold-and-emerald form bursting with predatory energy. The unfortunate animals who shared his space were quickly eaten, and a succession of damselfly larvae, minnows, newtpoles, tadpoles, water-boatman and lesser beetles fell to his rapacious appetite. The creature simply ate whatever he bumped into, except in the case of his favourite food, the lesser water beetles, which he would chase at high speed until not one remained. Louis kept a second jar with no *dytiscus*, and here a variety of other creatures lived in more security. One of these, the water-boatman, was in the habit of drawing attention to itself by rubbing its front limbs together and making a chirking noise, clearly audible from several yards away and evidently part of its mating ritual.

Our garden burn was also showing autumnal changes. The summer's growth of sedge-grass had obscured it so complete-ly that it took a close look to reveal the little overgrown pools with their gardens of aquatic plants tucked along its course. The year's trout fry had now reached three to four inches, and soon the burn's little run of mature trout would be making their way upstream to spawn in a gravel patch above the garden.

One creature which appeared in September, though with-out any apparent relation to the season, was a big adder. Leila and Sarah, two of the younger children, had been crossing a small field between houses when they came across the snake making its way across the open space. Having been well warned about such mythical beasts, they left it alone and came to report its presence to me. Adders are rare on the farm, and I was not convinced of its presence until the girls took me into the middle of the field where a long, dark shape on the grass dispelled all doubt. A very large female adder raised her head on our approach and watched coolly as I made plans for its soonest possible extermination. I had decided that a large rock would be the weapon, but as I moved away to find one something about the snake's head caught my eye. Sure enough, the oddly contrasting yellow of its underjaw identi-fied it as Yellowmouth, the same snake I had been studying for the past two years. Unable to decide what to do, I got the big rock anyway, but instead of dropping it on the adder I used it to hold down an overturned plastic bathtub which I put over her while I went away to settle her fate.

I decided that rather than kill her I would let her go on some distant moor. Since I also wanted to study her, I put her in a plastic jar on my desk, and for the next nine days she kept a beady red eye on me as I worked. I ended up by simply taking her back to her spruce tree in the forest, where she has remained ever since.

CHAPTER NINE

Season's End

A series of sharp frosts in mid-September had a sudden and dramatic effect on the appearance of the hills. Their vegetation turned, and the fading greens of late summer were largely replaced by contrasting shades of yellow, orange, brown and red. Each plant seemed to have a new colour as heather, bracken, sedge, and a multitude of bright grasses combined to give the landscape its autumn dress. When in the final week of the month rainstorms brought out the full brightness of colour, I decided to combine a last fishing trip with a walk in the hills.

Autumn journeys in the wilder parts of Scotland are a regular feature for some of the people at the farm. Bill usually manages a few days in the hills at this time, often in the company of myself or Angus, a migratory friend who also spends long winter months in the solitude of the high places. The satisfaction derived from these trips is not necessarily related to their duration, however, and when in the last days of September Angus and I set off for a one-night stay up the Bow Burn valley, we had all the expectations of explorers venturing into another world.

Low clouds were still sweeping over the moors after a day of south-westerly rain, and it was already evening by the time we left the farm, walking up past the wind-patterned length of Goose Island pool and turning onto a forest track towards the lower slopes of Dodd Hill. At its base the track splits and we took the left fork which would lead us around the north end of the hill, and up the Bow Burn valley. Above us, the pale rocky outcrops which stand up on the angle of the hill contrasted with the brown heather and the late green of the big bilberry patches at their bases. This part of the hill is a favourite haunt of predatory birds; one snowy mid-winter's day I watched four of them – a pair of kestrels and a pair of short-eared owls – in aerial combat over the slopes, the small animal which was the subject of their dispute passing in mid-air from one bird to another.

We followed the track around the corner and down across the Laggeran Burn, the first of the Bow Burn tributaries on our route, and continued up along the edge of Laggeran Hill. To our left, the conifers dropped away towards the bottom of the valley, and we could see the water of the Bow Burn running white with spate. A deer appeared ahead of us and bounded off into the trees as in the gathering dusk we followed the deteriorating track to the boggy moss patches at its end. Here we passed over the Poltribuie Burn and followed a broad windbreak leading up between stunted conifers towards the forest fence at the foot of the Cairnsmore.

Crossing here onto the easier ground beyond we stopped to drink at the Polchiffer, the third tributary of the Bow Burn coming off the Cairnsmore. This little torrent falls steeply down from the high boulder fields and, being untainted by the peaty influence of burns flowing through forest or bog its sweet water is a welcome treat for the walker. The open flanks of the Cairnsmore made easier going than the treacherous furrows of the forest, and after crossing the swollen Polchiffer we moved on rapidly towards the bouldery ridge below the mountain's north-eastern shoulder. From here we could see down to the small open plain which leads across to the Clennoch, our destination for the night, although the place itself was already invisible in the gathering darkness. Below us we could make out the Bow Burn, running now at several times its normal size, whose white water we would have to cross. The only likely place was a rocky section to our left and here, with the help of our staves, we were able to leap over the torrent from one big boulder to another. We were reminded of the difficulties faced by Gaberlunzie men, the itinerant wanderers of the past centuries who travelled these hills in all weathers, as well as the hardy clanspeople who lived in them.

The Clennoch was now little more than half a mile away, and we knew that by following the low ridge beyond the burn we would soon be there. On approaching it we came down again to the water to check out a long pool whose trout would hopefully provide our main meal of the morrow. It was now dark, but we located the spot without difficulty and ascertained that the floods of the previous winter had left it intact. We were about to move on when Angus noticed some glowing sparks appearing in the water of a nearby runnel as he placed his staff there before crossing over. I joined him and found that when I also ran a staff over the stream-bed tiny balls of

Carsphairn Church

118

glow-worm-like light materialized and drifted downstream, though more slowly, it seemed, than the fast-flowing water. I took the staff from the stream and was running the end of it over the bank-side grass to clean it when an odd thing happened. As the tip touched down the ground seemed to catch fire and a broad swathe of light followed the stick's course across the grass. I struck the ground again, and another bank of fire appeared, a thousand tiny lights sparking and spreading until it seemed as if the very hills were alight with unearthly fire. As we watched, a single large ball of light detached itself from the glowing mass and moved over to the staff. It hovered a few inches away and then began to spiral upwards around it; when I moved the stick it followed slowly after. This was not the last strange effect of this unexpected light show, however, for as we turned to go Angus left behind him a perfect set of fiery footprints, and for the final hundred yards to the Clennoch our boots and staves threw off a diminishing trail of sparks.

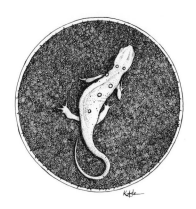

Of the many fine cottages whose remains now litter the Galloway hills, the Clennoch is one of the few which have not fallen into complete ruin, for a single small room has been saved and restored by the efforts of the Mountain Bothy Association in co-operation with its owner. It lies, however, in a part of the hills remote from popular hiking routes and this together with its small size have led to its being infrequently visited. Angus and I found a great bed of nettles growing across the doorway, and it looked as if few people had been there this year. Inside, the simple interior looked dry and comfortable; we deposited our bags there and went out to collect some wood while the rain, which had conveniently slackened off during our hike, began to gust in again. Nearby we found some rotting timbers from the old cottage which we split to obtain the dry wood inside, and these proved sufficient for the small fire which is so essential a part of a congenial stay in the hills.

A few stones were arranged into a fireplace near the door, and a metal teapot filled with water from the nearby Clennoch Burn was soon humming over the flame. We lit a candle in the room and, on doing so, discovered that we were not alone. In the middle of the floor sat a plump yellow newt, which I picked up and deposited safely under the sleeping-platform, marvelling at the creature's good fortune in having escaped annihilation under our heavy boots in the darkness. After tea we ate a simple meal of flat bread baked on the fireside stones, followed by more tea, before laying out our sleeping gear and turning in for the night to the music of the rain clattering on the roof.

We awoke as the dawn light was brightening the skylight above. 'Good day,' said Angus, and his comment was answered by the loud and resonant honk of a raven just outside. The bird's response was shortly followed by a gust of rain hitting the roof; though the day was indeed to be a good one, it was not to be on account of the weather. We rose and began the pleasant rituals of the morning: cutting wood and making the fire, drawing water from the burn and mixing dough for a breakfast of hot bread and sweet tea.

The meal over, Angus went out to gather more fuel while I made preparations to capture our midday meal. Putting up my long cane rod, I tied an equal-length piece of nylon line to the tip ring, adding a size-twelve hook and lead shot to complete the outfit, and after collecting a few worms from under the stones outside I set off between showers for the Bow Burn.

Low clouds were racing above the steep north face of the Cairnsmore which rose on the far side of the spating burn. Along the banks a line of sedge still showed green against the bleached yellow grasses, and I moved in near the head of the long pool where we had stopped the previous evening to cast my line into the fast, coloured water. A trout immediately took the bait, but the hook pulled free, and after several more bites I succeeded in landing only one wee fish. The trout at this end of the pool appeared to be too small to get the bait down, but as I moved on behind the protective line of sedge I began to contact larger ones. I spent half an hour making my way along the deeper water towards the tail of the pool and, as the rain blew in again, I caught half a dozen seven- and eight-inchers which together were enough to make up our meal. After gutting the catch by the burn, I returned to the Clennoch and spread the fish out in preparation for baking on a slab of slate laid across the fire.

In better weather we would have taken a walk to look at some of the sights of the Cairnsmore, whose stony screes we could see from the door, or Windy Standard, the lesser mountain which rose behind us. In the continuing rain, however, we were content to leave visitations to Luke's Stone, the Devil's Putting Stone, or the mysterious Roaring Cleugh to other days. We had plenty to do around the bothy and after lunch busied ourselves with minor improvements to the room, collecting firewood for future visitors, making tea and taking photographs of nearby views. At one point a meadow-pipit which had been taking an interest in our activities since our arrival joined us in the bothy and sat for some time watching us work. We saw no further sign of the raven which had been with us at dawn and apart from the pipit and a pair of chaffinches the only other birds we saw were some carrion crows and a couple of red grouse skimming low over the distant moor. There had once been ptarmigan on the Cairns-more, but snipe, grouse, and the occasional blackcock are now the only game birds to be seen here. There may once have been resident eagles on the Cairnsmore too, but in recent years few have been seen in the area. A lone eagle spent a few weeks on the mountain one winter, and Davy McKay had a fine sighting of it when, walking the upper slopes in a heavy mist, he surprised it sitting on a rock. My wife saw another one as I was working on the final chapter of this book. Probably one of the Mulwarchar pair, it circled several times around Bow Craig, the site of an old village above the confluence of the Bow Burn and the Deugh, before heading off towards the Rhinns.

Around the Clennoch smaller birds are often unusually curious about a human presence. In the summer several species are present in the area and they may crowd around the visitor with little fear. On a lone trip one August, my every move was followed by a spellbound audience of some two dozen pipits sitting on the roof and every available boulder round about. A robin perched feet away from the fire, and when I went down to the burn for water a family of swallows skimmed low over my head. Two kinds of mammals also appeared on that visit. On my arrival a weasel had watched me from the crumbling walls nearby, which, when I squeaked at it, stood up among the stones and showed its long white underside. At dusk on the following evening I was fishing a fly along the Bow Burn when a roe deer appeared and barked at me until I left. This part of the hills is renowned for foxes, and on one visit to Windy Standard I watched one hunting voles on the summit.

On another occasion I took a walk over Windy Standard to see the source of the Deugh. The day was very hot, the sun shining from a cloudless sky as I followed the Clennoch Burn up behind the bothy. Small fish sped away across the little

A fox hunting a vole on the summit of Windy Standard; beyond lie the steep north-eastern slopes of Moorbrock Hill (left), Beninner and Cairnsmore.

pools at my approach; at one point I found a surprisingly large and heavily spotted trout poised in the current below an overhanging fern. I climbed for a mile or so to the burn's source and up onto the watershed, where a dramatic vista opened up. From the rim of Windy Standard's eastern scarp, above the steep screes known as the Blue Stones, I had a fine south-eastern view down the beautiful glen of the Holm Burn to the green spot which marked the Nether Holm of Dalquhairn in the valley of the Ken. From the summit more dramatic views appeared, and in addition to the steep gairies of the Cairnsmore, Benina and Moorbrock Hill to the south, the more distant peaks of the Rhinns were clearly visible to the south-west. In the north-east a dark patch of coniferous forest marked the location of Afton Reservoir, while to the north-west the big hills dropped away towards the hazy lowlands of Scotland's Central Belt.

I found the source of the Deugh at the head of a small gulley on the far side of the peak. Three watery trickles joined together in a small sedge bog, and below it the young Deugh fell away loudly towards the valley floor. Not far from the source the river ran into the big conifer plantations which flank most of its course; as I moved down the stream a pair of red deer hinds bounded up a windbreak and disappeared over a high ridge. At the foot of the slope the tiny waterway was joined by another, and a few yards below the confluence I saw the first trout. There were two fish lying in a tiny pool, pale ones with heavily spotted backs which looked surprisingly large for the new fry I had expected to see this far upstream. They lay curled up in the open, and their pool was so small that I was able to catch one easily in my cupped hands and take a closer look at it. The exquisitely marked fish certainly seemed, at four inches long, to be an exceptional size for that year's generation, and as I slipped the trout back into the water I wondered if these two were already in their second year. Later that day I noticed that the smallest fish in the upper Bow Burn were only around two and a half inches long, a more typical size for August fry, but since these too had very pale backs and lay out in the open in the same way I concluded that the pair I had seen near the Deugh source were in fact unusually well-fed first-summer fish.

I once made another walk with Bill over Windy Standard in weather conditions very different to that high-summer day. It was in November, and a biting north-easterly wind offset the warmth of a hazy sun as we left the farm. We had planned a hike across the trackless country beyond Windy Standard, and on stopping for tea at the Clennoch, some five miles out, we noticed cloud gathering on the heights above. In spite of the ominous weather we decided to keep going, but by the time we reached the ridge at the head of the Clennoch Burn the sun was disappearing and we found ourselves walking into a thickening blizzard. We slowly followed the steep ridge above the Blue Stones; once or twice the curtain of falling snow parted to expose a view as impressive as the mountains of Antarctica. In the hours which followed we were also to find ourselves encountering the sort of physical problems which may be faced by visitors to that polar continent.

We found our way off Windy Standard without difficulty, crossed the Afton Water near its source, and climbed the south edge of Alwhat towards Cloud Hill. Ahead lay the lonely glens which wind down towards the Nith, but as we crossed the watershed, a long hill-end from which four streams rise, we began to feel the effects of the hard weather. Enough snow was now lying on the rough ground to make walking difficult, and we found that the food we had with us for the trip, which would have sufficed in most other weather conditions, was not sufficient to replace the energy we were losing by hard walking in the intense cold. On reaching the upper part of the Euchan glen we found the slopes recently ploughed, the hazardous ditches of this unexpected forest extension adding to our difficulties. After an hour of crossing them both of us were suffering from exhaustion and we were relieved to reach the ruin of Euchanhead, some fifteen miles out from the start of our walk.

That night snow continued falling and we awoke to find it thick on the ground. By mid-morning the snow had stopped and we set out on the final few miles of our journey. The track which starts at the ruin made the going easier, although as we waded through the drifts the grim atmosphere which had prevailed since our entry to the glen remained with us. Now, however, it was not our own condition which was the cause of it but the sad signs of the valley's recent past.

The first indications of the story had come the previous day when we saw the great scars of the new ploughing at the head of the glen. The furrows continued down both sides, then came the remains of human habitation. Euchanhead, like many another remote cottage, had obviously been deserted for some years before the forestry arrived, but the dereliction of the next house had been more recent and, though still in good condition, this one had been used to stable animals. The next one, two miles further on, was still inhabited but the lack of grazing land round about showed that its days as a centre of herding were already over. Near the mouth of the glen, the inevitable forest gate barred the road; the suspicious gazes of people crowding the window of the house nearby, and their failure to return our wave of greeting, was a fitting end to our glimpse of the sad story of the Euchan Glen – a tale of depopulation which could be told in similar fashion of so many other beautiful valleys throughout Scotland.

The unseemly haste with which the forestry concerns moved in, riding the wave of tax concessions and government aid, should have attracted far more attention than it has. Scotland, however, is the only country in Europe in which property owners are not required by law to register the use of

Kello, Euchan, Scaur and Ken
All rise out of one hill end

their land, so that local people have no say in the takeovers by city-based organizations which seem to ignore the warnings against monoculture expressed by the founding fathers of modern forestry. For the people whose land now adjoins the forest the changes have also meant new problems, as instead of being able to discuss matters of common concern as they would with a neighbouring farmer, they find that the only real decision-makers in the forestry firms are businessmen or bureaucrats living hundreds of miles away. The resulting unsatisfactory relationships have now led to dangerous antagonism between the two main users of the land.

Meanwhile, the local people who have had the longest relationships with the hills find their visits barred increasingly by forest gates. In Dalmellington, the mining town which over the years has received many of the people leaving the Galloway hills, the intensity of interest in hill-walking, natural history and fishing is quite remarkable, as is the number of individuals who reflect their feelings for the traditions of the area in verse and story. It is a sad indication of the state of society that those who would most dearly love a more direct relationship with the hills of their forebears have so little possibility of realizing it.

The process of rural depopulation has been going on in Scotland for over two centuries, and it is happening now throughout the world. Its cause no doubt lies in the changing view of land as the basis of individual wealth and sustenance. and as people leave to make a living in the industrial centres it falls into the hands of fewer owners. Meanwhile, the rigid concept of enclosures and the loss of common grazing ground have made it increasingly difficult for anyone of ordinary material means to regain the relationship with the land which their ancestors took for granted. It is an odd fact, though, that even those who are content to spend their lives in the city still regard the country life as an ideal on which to base a family existence relatively free from the totalitarianism which, under every political colour, still dominates world ideology.

Scotland, when compared to some countries, is still relatively well off, for in spite of an often unimaginative use of the land its people retain a strong sense of personal identity. Nevertheless, the pressures of modern life are showing, and today there are few people who are prepared to face the hard existence of Bert MacAdam and his wife, the last residents of the Clennoch.

Angus and I had a refreshing taste of Bert MacAdam's existence, and perhaps that of his forebears as well, on our autumn walk to the Clennoch. The south-westerly wind would have been familiar to all who had lived there, for it brought with it the wild, wet conditions so typical of the Galloway hills. By the end of our day we had become so absorbed in the atmosphere of the lonely glen that we no longer noticed the wind and weather, nor even the time of day; and once again dusk was drawing in by the time we came to gather our few belongings and head off through the rain towards the white line of the burn.